RESTORING PERSONS IN WORLD COMMUNITY

RESTORING PERSONS IN WORLD COMMUNITY

By

J. Andrew Bolton

Zionic Relations Office
Reorganized Church of Jesus Christ of Latter Day Saints
Herald Publishing House

Library of Congress Cataloging-in-Publication Data

Bolton, J. Andrew.
Restoring Persons in World Community.

1. Sociology, Christian (Mormon) 2. Reorganized Church of Jesus Christ of Latter Day Saints—Doctrines.
I. Title.
BX8675.B65 1986 261.8 86-20134
ISBN 0-8309-0461-1

89 88 87 86 2 3 4 5 6 7 8

With respect and thanks to my parents
and three brothers who first taught
me something about equal worth
and the importance of justice.

Also to John Menzies who
first told me about the kingdom.

CONTENTS

The Kingdom of God has only love by which it can achieve its purposes; and the only instrument which love knows by which it can achieve its purpose is sacrifice.

—Arthur Oakman, *He Who Is*

PREFACE

The Restoration movement contains many powerful insights within its history and its doctrines. From the richness of our tradition we glean those ideas and insights which guide and sustain us in the present and the future. Nowhere is this more true than in relation to our concept of community and the worth of persons living in community.

For most of us it is difficult to speak in a prophetic voice and to ask the hard questions in a world fraught with problems. It remains for isolated individuals, then, to speak when others are silent, to act while others watch, to step forward with a unique way of perceiving and understanding who we are—as a people and a church—to testify in ways which affirm and challenge us. J. Andrew Bolton is such a person; *Restoring Persons in World Community* is such a testimony.

This book is the culmination of nearly twenty years' work to place experiences and insights into a particular perspective, a Restoration perspective. It is addressed to all who have come to cherish the uniqueness of our movement, and yet, who also feel the need to broaden this circle of concern and understanding to encompass needs outside the church. For these persons, the cause of Zion does not involve an attempt to build "Restoration communities" apart from the world's tumult. Rather, Zion is a cause to "restore persons" into a world community wherein they feel a oneness, a kinship in trial and triumph, and a call to make our world a better place for our children and their children.

Andrew Bolton's touchstone of morality—the welfare of children—is simple, yet profound. His belief that whatever benefits the welfare of children benefits all of us is similar to Jesus saying that "of such is the kingdom of heaven." At the root of this approach is the conviction that to build the kingdom is to build a better world for our children where they can feel secure and accepted, challenged and nurtured. This, surely, is a worthy goal of the cause of Zion, and one upon which the process of "restoration" must focus.

Justice is another vital theme in the restoration of persons. Charity is an essential element in the life of any community, but unless charity is rooted in the ancient and biblical concern for justice, it does not go far enough. Bolton believes that none of us is equal unless we are all equal. When one of our number is dealt with unjustly or as having lesser worth, we are all diminished. We are living in a time in which our natural resources are distributed unequally, some persons are treated in dehumanizing ways, and the tools of war have higher priority than the development of vital human communities. This is unjust, at best; demonic, at worst. Thus, we are all challenged to rectify conditions like these and to draw upon our own heritage—where our ancestors were victims of injustice—to fashion for our sisters and brothers today a world that is more fulfilling for all.

Finally, the Restoration movement has often been concerned with peace, but has not been a peace movement. Yet we are uniquely qualified to be a peace church and to bring alive the biblical image which is our symbol—where the lion and the lamb shall lie down together with the child. That child represents all of us. It is our best hope for the future. It symbolizes our best attempts to deal with the forces of war and destruction in our world and to beat "swords into plowshares." This child is the focus of our ministries of reconciliation and caring: to earnestly attempt to love our enemies and to remember that we are sisters and brothers with God as our common creator.

Restoring Persons in World Community bears a hopeful message. Conceived in experiences of cross-cultural learning and sharing, it is offered as a bridge between people who are different and ideas which are diverse. It can be a tool for new meaning and increased understanding. It can be a way to hold up our tradition much as we would hold up a prism and allow a source of light to penetrate it and cast new rays of light into many directions. It may enable us to take an important step on a path to new understanding and new commitment. I commend this book—and its author—to you with such hopes, and with a final hope that our growing relations with other persons in our world may become increasingly redemptive, compassionate, just, and "Zionic."

Robert E. Kent
for the Zionic Relations Office

INTRODUCTION

The *worth of persons* is a major commitment of the Restoration movement, derived from God's awesome commitment to us in sacrificial love. If we ever wonder whether God is for us or against us we need only turn to the cross of Good Friday and the restoration of Easter morning.

The worth of persons has found expression in different and significant ways in Restoration history for over 150 years. Sadly, Jewish people in European history have been the most despised of people. To many European settlers in the New World, the native Americans were merely savages to be exterminated. Both Jews and native Americans were affirmed by the Book of Mormon as part of God's people and, therefore, of special worth. The emphasis on common consent in the church recognizes, in another way, the worthwhile contribution of each to sense rightness and make decisions. The calling of men of humble origins—red, yellow, black, and white—to be ministers for Christ was an affirmation of the worth and giftedness inherent in those who were not privileged in worldly opportunities. The equal calling of women to be ministers is also but a rightful application of the worth and giftedness of all persons. The early emphasis on economic equality—in terms of consumption and need—was yet another expression of the equal worth of persons. Education has been important from the beginning of the Restoration because it allows human abilities to grow, thus enabling human worth to be more fully realized.

It has always been a central affirmation of the Restoration that human worth is most fully realized in community. The vision of those early pioneers of our faith affirmed that people truly *are* and know a fullness of joy in righteous and whole communities. Thus community building involving politics, economics, architecture, and spiritual concerns was the primary thrust and melody of early Restoration Christians. They called it Zion, the kingdom of God coming on earth. The communities they founded suffered from human frailties, but nevertheless expressed a vision of possibility—when humans come together to consecrate all aspects of their lives to God.

The world we now live in is very different from the 1830s. Theirs was primarily an agricultural world. Since then our world has gone through an Industrial Revolution and is now entering the Information Age. With many new human institutions and systems, the world has become an interconnected whole. New opportunities for realizing human worth in global community now exist. Also existing are the frightening possibilities of continued poverty for billions and nuclear holocaust for all of us.

In this book I attempt to begin applying the worth of persons and community vision to our day. Specific emphasis is on hunger and violence, two major betrayals of human worth and community.

In many ways, my own pilgrimage is expressed in this book. My interest in the world's food problem stems from a geography lesson at age seventeen. It led to university degrees in horticulture and agricultural botany. At first I thought hunger was a technological problem, a matter simply of producing more food. But then I grew wiser and gradually became aware of the economic, political, cultural, historical, and spiritual dimensions underlying poverty.

While in my early twenties, I discovered the Restoration movement, first in West Germany and later in Wales. There came, after much questioning and listening, conversion and commitment to Christ and his kingdom purposes. It has been the best decision I have ever made.

Then came the peaceable and joyful influence of Jewell Holmes into my life. We shared a sense of mission that eventually resulted in a marriage covenant. It was during our four busy years in Oxford, employed as teachers and involved as leaders in a local congregation, that the germ of this book emerged as we sought to express the relevancy of the Restoration movement in that place.

"Out of the blue" in 1981 came the gracious invitation from Kisuke Sekine to work for two years in Japan. There we met Hiroshi Yamada, Hiroshi Matsushita, and Dayle Bethel. They opened up a whole new world for us. Through Dayle Bethel's intercultural center in Osaka, I researched and gave seminars on world hunger. During this time I began to see for the first time the connection between hunger, poverty, and military spending. Thus I became interested not only in world hunger but also world peace. Then came the opportunity to spend a year of intensive studies at Temple School and Park College in Independence, Missouri. Here, in the study of the Bible, Christian history, and Restoration history and theology, I was challenged to be more cautious and more thorough in my scholarship. During this time staff of the Zionic Relations Office proposed this book. In its completion I owe debts to many but especially to my two young boys and Jewell, from whom time was stolen to research and write. Even though twenty years of study, experience, and reflection are contained in this book, I am still learning. While my conclusions may be more cautious than in times past, no doubt they will always need further modification. What is offered, then, is one attempt to apply human worth and community in our day.

For many years I wallowed in guilt, despair, and helplessness. This book reflects these feelings and the anger that can be generated from perceived injustice and human foolishness. However, this book also includes expressions of my emerging, cautious optimism and my grounds for hope in the prophetic task that belongs to all who have sensed the calling of God's Spirit. The prophetic task has always been the restoring of persons to the wholeness of right relationships with God and with each other. To this task God invites, beckons, and calls our generation. These are portentous and perilous times and we need to understand that very clearly. But we also need to recognize that God's purpose for our world is life, and life abundant. It is joy, and joy in all its fullness. A great and marvelous work is indeed about to come forth. I hope and pray that a glimpse of that conviction will be seen by those who study this book.

J. Andrew Bolton
Leicester, England
August 1985

With righteousness he shall judge the poor, and decide with equity for the meek of the earth.

—Isaiah 11:4 Revised Standard Version

And the Lord called his people, Zion, because they were of one heart and of one mind, and dwelt in righteousness; and there were no poor among them.

—Genesis 7:23 Inspired Version

The Christian who is poor must be glad when God lifts him up, and the rich Christian must be glad when God brings him down. For the rich will pass away like the flower of a wild plant.

—James 1:9-10 Today's English Version

CHAPTER 1
RESTORING EQUALITY

The Old Testament Story

In the beginning there was equality. Eve was made from the rib of Adam, not from his head to be above him, nor from his foot to be stepped on, but from his side to be equal with him. It was only after the fall that Eve was told, "Your desire shall be for your husband and he shall rule over you" (Genesis 3:16 RSV). Inequality is a consequence of the fall. It was not so in the beginning.

Although we might be content with our fallen inequality, especially if we fell landing on top, the biblical testimony is that God was not. This is seen clearly in Israel's slavery in Egypt. God confronted Moses and said:

> I have seen the affliction of my people who are in Egypt, and have heard their cry because of their taskmasters; I know their sufferings, and I have come down to deliver them out of the hand of the Egyptians, and to bring them up out of that land to a good and broad land, a land flowing with milk and honey.—Exodus 3:7, 8 RSV

Why was God telling Moses? It was because Moses was part of God's plan of restoring equality: "Come, I will send you to Pharaoh that you may bring forth my people, the sons of Israel, out of Egypt" (Exodus 3:10 RSV). Thus we have the beginning of the Exodus story.

The book of Exodus has been described as standing in relationship to the Old Testament in the same way that the Gospels are to the New Testament. The event of Exodus is to Israel what Resurrection is to Christianity. Indeed, the Exodus theme, the restoration to whole relationships of equality, is a theme found again and again in the biblical story.

We meet another "exodus" in Sinai when the Law was given through Moses to the people of Israel. They were not to re-create in the promised land the injustices of the Egyptian society they had just left. The law given was to create and maintain a society covenanted to equality, a society where "you shall love your neighbor as yourself" (Leviticus 19:18 RSV). Thus Sinai is a second "exodus" to fulfill the first, the escape from Egypt and from inequality.

If Israelites were indeed to be equal, then they must not only be free from slavery but have equal access to making a living. In an agricultural society, land is essential for the vast majority of the population. Read what God told Moses about land: "Divide the land among the tribes, according to their size. Divide the land by drawing lots, and give a large share to a larger tribe and a smaller one to a smaller tribe" (Numbers 25:53-56 TEV).

This was not all. Not only were the Israelites to start out free and equal, they were to stay that way. One is impressed by the earthly realism of the law as providing regulations to achieve this. It would be natural for some in Israel to fall upon hard times, to lose land, and even to be sold into slavery to pay debts. The law, however, provided for this, in the Sabbath-year regulations—to restore equality. The Sinai covenant stated: "When you buy a Hebrew slave, he shall serve you six years and in the seventh he shall go free for nothing" (Exodus 21:2 RSV).

They were also to be given sheep, goats, grain, and wine as aid for a new start (Deuteronomy 15:12-15). Also in the same passage in Deuteronomy, debts were to be forgiven in the seventh year (Deuteronomy 15:1-11), again a means to restore equality.

The Year of Restoration, more commonly called the Jubilee Year, was the capstone of the sabbatical-year regulations. It was concerned with maintaining the original, equal distribution of land among the Israelites when they entered the Promised Land.

The Year of Restoration

Count seven times seven years, a total of forty-nine years. Then, on the tenth day of the seventh month, the Day of Atonement, send a man to blow a trumpet throughout the whole land. In this way you shall set the fiftieth year apart and proclaim freedom to all the inhabitants of the land. During this year all property that has been sold shall be restored to the original owner or his descendants, and anyone who has been sold as a slave shall return to his family.—Leviticus 25:8-10, 13 TEV

This remarkable legislation was intended to prevent some farmers from becoming extraordinarily wealthy and others, by their own errors or through difficult times, becoming landless and leaving their families permanently destitute.

This special year has been described as "Exodus spelled out in terms of social salvation."[1] The Year of Jubilee was, therefore, an attempt to institutionalize the Exodus event in settlement in the Promised Land, so that *exodus* would be a continuing process in the life of the people of Israel. The processes that made slavery and inequality were to be continually and regularly overcome. The Jubilee Year was thus rooted in the Sinai Covenant, the new way of life, grounded in God (Yahweh) for the people of Israel.

The Jubilee Year and the other sabbatical-year regulations for the release of slaves and debts continued to inspire the prophetic imagination in the later history of Israel. In the difficult times of Babylonian exile and in anticipation of restoration to their homeland, the themes of Jubilee restoration and sabbatical-year release were reworked in the prophetic passages of Isaiah, especially Isaiah 58:6 and 61:1. Both in Hebrew and in Greek, the same words are used in Isaiah, Leviticus, and Deuteronomy for liberty and release. Scholars have demonstrated that at the time of Jesus the hopes described in Isaiah 61:1 would have been commonly understood in terms of Jubilee restoration of land and sabbatical release of debts and slaves.[2] This makes Jesus' famous reading of Isaiah 61:1 in Nazareth, as recorded in Luke 4:18, 19, tremendously significant.

Jesus and the Restoration of Equality

In the first chapter of Mark, Jesus is described as beginning his ministry with the kingdom message: "Now after John was arrested, Jesus came into Galilee, preaching the gospel of God, and saying, 'The time is fulfilled, and the kingdom of God is at hand; repent, and believe in the gospel'" (Mark 1:14-15 RSV). Excited as I was with the kingdom of God message in the first days after my baptism, I nevertheless wondered what Jesus meant by preaching the "kingdom of God." All that is found in Mark is the theme of Jesus' preaching, not the content of his sermons. I longed to hear Jesus preach the message of the kingdom of God. What would he say?

Then I read in Luke about Jesus preaching at the beginning of his ministry in his home village of Nazareth. The text includes Jesus reading from Isaiah, a sermon outline, and the reaction of the congregation:

> And he came to Nazareth, where he had been brought up; and he went to the synagogue, as his custom was, on the sabbath day. And he stood up to read: and there was given to him the book of the prophet Isaiah. He opened the book and found the place where it was written, "The Spirit of the Lord is upon me, because

he has anointed me to preach good news to the poor. He has sent me to proclaim release to the captives and recovering of sight to the blind, to set at liberty those who are oppressed, to proclaim the acceptable year of the Lord." And he closed the book, and gave it back to the attendant, and sat down; and the eyes of all in the synagogue were fixed upon him. And he began to say to them, "Today this scripture has been fulfilled in your hearing." And all spoke well of him, and wondered at the gracious words which proceeded out of his mouth; and they said, "Is not this Joseph's son?"—Luke 4:16-22 RSV

The text Jesus chose is from Isaiah 61:1/58:6, the very passages linked with release of debts, release of slaves, and restoration of land to the original owners. At the beginning of his ministry Jesus is pictured by Luke returning to the ancient melody of exodus and the restoration of equality. That is why it was good news to the poor, the captives, the physically handicapped, and the oppressed. Jesus identified himself quite clearly with the prophetic tradition of his people.

In reading "to proclaim the acceptable year of the Lord" Jesus was saying today—this year—is the Jubilee Year, the year of restoring equality of property. In saying "Today this scripture is fulfilled in your hearing" Jesus was saying that he was the Messiah, the One anointed by the Spirit of the Lord to initiate the new age when equality shall be restored.

Why was the Nazareth congregation later so angry with him? Was it because Jesus went on to imply that the Jubilee Age was to include not only them but Gentiles also? Possibly. Or was it really because the people of wealth in the congregation were threatened by a preacher who was announcing that the Jubilee Age of restored equality had come?[3] The notion of equality has frequently angered the privileged.

The Jubilean motif is found elsewhere in the Gospels. It has been argued that the Lord's prayer is a Jubilee prayer in which we cancel debts owed us by the poor because God has cancelled our debts.[4] The parable of the unjust steward (Luke 16:1-9) becomes meaningful when interpreted with a Jubilee perspective.[5] The story of the rich young ruler is the story of one who sorrowfully could not let go of his property in a Jubilee release. Zachaeus, on the other hand, enthusiastically embraces "the great movement of Jubilean reform undertaken by Jesus."[6]

New light is thrown on the struggle of Jesus with the Pharisees over the Sabbath. Jesus' argument was that the Sabbath institution was made for liberation from debts, captivity, and the return to equality; it was not an institution of petty oppressive regulations concerning work and rest.[7]

In Matthew the Sermon on the Mount is seen as a Jubilee speech.[8] Again in Matthew, chapter 25, the judgment of the nations is depicted in a way which remarkably parallels the Isaiah text Jesus read in Luke 4:18. We shall be held accountable, according to Matthew 25, for feeding the hungry, giving water to the thirsty, clothing the naked, visiting those in prison, visiting the sick, and welcoming the stranger.[9] Thus on the day of judgment we shall be held accountable as to whether social exodus, that is, the Jubilean restoration of equality, has been lived out in our lives.

The Crucifixion is full of the symbols of exodus—deliverance from the oppression of sin through Christ our Passover. The theme of social exodus in the year of Restoration/Jubilee is also clearly seen in the cross. The Crucifixion, the Day of Atonement and the Jubilee/Restoration proclamation of liberty to be trumpeted throughout the whole world to all its inhabitants, is foreshadowed in Leviticus 25:8-10. The cross is thus restored by this perspective to an instrument not only of personal salvation but also of social salvation. We are to be saved from poverty and uncaring affluence as well as from guilt.

Is it any wonder that early Christians shared their material resources in Jerusalem? One scholar has commented: "For the first Christians . . . the expectation of the restoration of all things required an immediate application of Moses' sabbatical teaching [including the year of Restoration/Jubilee] interpreted by Jesus."[10]

Paul, in organizing collections among Gentile Christians for poverty-stricken Jerusalem Christians, appeals to the Corinthians as follows: "For you know the grace of our Lord Jesus Christ, that though he was rich, yet for your sake he became poor, so that by his poverty you might become rich" (II Corinthians 8:9 RSV). Jesus sets a personal example for Paul that exceeds even the requirements of the Jubilee/Restoration theology of the Old Testament. Paul's point to the Corinthians, however, is equality: "I do not mean that others should be eased and you burdened, but that as a matter of equality your abundance at the present time should supply their want, so that their abundance may supply your want, that there may be equality" (II Corinthians 8:13-14 RSV).

The Later Church

Throughout its history, the church has continued to teach believers to use wealth as a stewardship for the sake of the poor. For more than a thousand years, a Christianity which in other ways may have fallen sadly from its noble beginnings earnestly attempted to regulate economics and social institutions for the protection of the poor and the vulnerable. With the development of trade and finance in sixteenth-century Europe, however, the church's understanding of economics remained largely of a previous age. The church's thinking did not keep up with the times. The Reformation saw most of the Protestant tradition over the next two centuries make a separation between spiritual and secular so that economics was no longer judged and held accountable by the Bible or the church's social tradition. By abandoning its prophetic function in calling all of life to be under the Lordship of Christ, both Catholic and Protestant churches betrayed the poor and vulnerable to the forces of greed permitted by the development of markets, competition, and machines in the Industrial Revolution.

However, some Christians in post-Reformation Europe, persecuted and driven, saw in the recently discovered New World a promised land, an opportunity to yet build the kingdom of God on earth. So in a new exodus pilgrims journeyed across the Atlantic to build a community under God.

The Restoration Movement

The Puritans in their New England towns had sought "social perfection and the possibility of realizing certain social values. Community life meant they could worship together, educate their children, and share their labor and equipment in open fields."[11]

Joseph Smith, Jr., and the majority of those who associated with him were of this New England background. Smith's culture was influenced by the Bible through his Puritan New England origins and contemporary revivals in the so-called "Burnt Over District" in New York State. Living at a time of "Owenite-utopian" experiments and different religious communitarianisms, it is not surprising Smith was interested in such ventures himself, particularly in view of his own poverty.

With reference to Smith's poverty, Flanders states:

> Smith felt himself an alienated youth, the product of an alienated family.... [The Smiths belonged] to the large company of Americans who were beyond the edge of successful genteel society and the institutional establishment of their time. And they were generally inclined to distrust the establishment whether its manifestations be theological, ecclesiological, political or economical.[12]

The Book of Mormon reflects the association of economic sharing and equality with religious conversion: The baptized believers "walked uprightly before God, imparting to one another, both temporally and spiritually, according to their needs and their wants."—Mosiah 9:64

> [Alma] saw great inequality among the people, some lifting themselves up with their pride, despising others, turning their backs upon the needy, and the naked, and those who were hungry, and those who were thirsty, and those who were sick and afflicted.—Alma 2:19

> And there was no inequality among them, for the Lord poured out his Spirit.—Alma 11:26

> Thus we see how great the inequality of man is because of sin and transgression, and the power of the devil which comes by the cunning plans which he has devised to ensnare the hearts of men.—Alma 15:50

> And as many as came to them and truly repented of their sins were baptized in the name of Jesus; and they also received the Holy Ghost....And they had all things common among them, therefore they were not rich and poor, bond and free, but they were all made free and partakers of the heavenly gift.—IV Nephi 1:2, 4

The opportunity to implement Joseph Smith's social and economic idealism came in early 1831. Sidney Rigdon and his experimental communities had joined the Mormons at the end of the previous year. On February 9, 1831, Smith presented a revelation outlining a new economic ethic:

> And behold, thou shalt consecrate all thy properties, that which thou hast unto me, with a covenant and a deed which cannot be broken; and they shall be laid before the bishop of my church, and two of the elders, such as he shall appoint and set apart for that purpose.
>
> And it shall come to pass, that the bishop of my church, after that he has received the properties of my church, that it cannot be taken from the church, he shall appoint every man a steward over his own property, or that which he has received, inasmuch as is sufficient for himself and family.
>
> And the residue shall be kept to administer to him who has not, that every man may receive according as he stands in need.
>
> And the residue shall be kept in my storehouse, to administer to the poor and needy, as shall be appointed by the elders of the church and the bishop; and for the purpose of purchasing lands, and the building up of the New Jerusalem, which is hereafter to be revealed; that my covenant people may be gathered in one, in the day that I shall come to my temple. And this I do for the salvation of my people.[13]

Joseph Smith's new economic ethic, intended to rescue Sidney Rigdon's "free-for-all" socialism, "was a prescription for transforming the highly individualistic economic order of Jacksonian America into a system characterized by economic equality, socialization of surplus income, freedom of enterprise and group economic self-sufficiency."[14]

Joseph Smith, Jr., was thus very clearly in the biblical tradition of restoring economic equality and adapted to the economic institutions of his age. It is interesting to note the frequent appeals for economic equality in revelations given in 1831 and 1832:

Let every man esteem his brother as himself; for what man among you having twelve sons, and is no respecter to them, and they serve him obediently, and he saith unto the one, Be thou clothed in robes and sit thou here; and to the other, Be thou clothed in rags and sit thou there, and looketh upon his sons and saith, I am just.—Doctrine and Covenants 38:5d

But it is not given that one man should possess that which is above another; wherefore the world lieth in sin.—Doctrine and Covenants 49:3e, f

Appoint unto this people their portion, every man equal according to their families, according to their circumstances, and their wants and needs.—Doctrine and Covenants 51:1b

Nevertheless, in your temporal things you shall be equal, and this not grudgingly, otherwise the abundance of the manifestations of the Spirit shall be withheld.—Doctrine and Covenants 70:3d

For if ye are not equal in earthly things, ye cannot be equal in obtaining heavenly things.—Doctrine and Covenants 77:1f

The new economic ethic given through Smith as the law of consecration and stewardship was designed remarkably for equality of consumption while enabling Saints of different abilities to have different and thus unequal responsibilities.[15]

There were problems with the working out of Smith's economic ethic in the law of consecration and stewardship, and in 1833 the whole experiment came to an abrupt and tragic end in Missouri with the expulsion of the Saints from Independence.

In 1838 at Far West, Missouri, another system was introduced using a tithing method after an initial consecration of surplus goods (Doctrine and Covenants 106).

This law of tithing, was introduced because "the people had polluted their inheritances" while in Jackson County. In principle, however, it was not greatly different from the so-called celestial law of 1831.[16]

Uprooted by violence again, the law of tithing was reintroduced in 1841 in Nauvoo. This law "contained no device for the reform of property institutions or for achieving a more equitable distribution of wealth and income."[17]

In Nauvoo, charity, or relief of the poor, was practiced rather than the earlier attempts to eliminate poverty by structural economic changes. Joseph Smith is, thus, most clearly in the biblical tradition of restoration of economic equality in the decade 1830-39. In Nauvoo Joseph Smith was content with a modified approach to church finances. Yet his followers in numerous factions after his assassination attempted to return to patterns of community designed to restore economic equality.

Joseph Smith was a contemporary of Owen and Marx, but in two important ways he was like neither of them. First, Zion—the New Jerusalem—was to be a Christian society, a converted society and a repentant society in response to the endowment of the Holy Spirit. Second, Joseph Smith never had to face industrial capitalism; neither did most of his followers in their various factions in the nineteenth century except for those escaping from industrial Europe to agrarian America.

Nineteenth-century Mormonism could in part be described as a community attempt of religious, poor people to survive in an agrarian setting. In some ways their world was much nearer the world of the Old Testament prophets than for those living in industrial capitalism in Europe.

By the end of the nineteenth century Mormonism had adapted to the dominant culture in America. The Reorganization perhaps adapted earlier than the more isolated Utah Mormonism. While the gospel and utopian idealism would remain alive in the thoughts of the Latter Day Saints, the churches had begun disengaging from serious attempts to change history.

In North America, the social gospel movement between 1880 and 1930 was influential and to a degree successful. Toughened by the criticism of the Niebuhrs and supplemented by Gandhism, the social gospel was alive and well in the civil rights movement and continues as a force in Christianity today.

Echoes of the social gospel are found combined with Restoration theology in the work of Frederick M. Smith, the first president of the RLDS Church to address industrial capitalism. He attempted to lead the church in applying its tradition of economic equality and community building to the twentieth century. A flavor of his thought can be gleaned from the following quotations:

> Large fortunes and luxury are possessed by a small class. . . . The strenuous legal efforts to safeguard private property rather than the general weal have completely upset equality of opportunity [so] that it is a bit farcical to claim its existence for all.[18]

> *Luxury is justified only when commonly enjoyed.* No Christian, well within the spiritual influence of the genius of his religion, can be happy in the midst of luxury as long as the knowledge remains that others have not the necessities of life.[19] (emphasis in original)

> The church must foster social reform, and its stalwarts may even have to enter politics to accomplish it. It must stand for social freedom, and this necessitates a break with present conditions, for the church must stand for wealth becoming pervasive and not the heritage of a privileged class.[20]

> The religion of Jesus is fundamentally social.[21]

Twice in recent years the church has been admonished to be in the forefront:

These are portentous times. The lives of many are being sacrificed unnecessarily to the gods of war, greed, and avarice. The land is being desecrated by the thoughtless waste of vital resources. You must obey my commandments and be in the forefront of those who would mediate this needless destruction while there is yet day.—Doctrine and Covenants 150:7

You who are my disciples must be found continuing in the forefront of those organizations and movements which are recognizing the worth of persons and are committed to bringing the ministry of my Son to bear on their lives.—Doctrine and Covenants 151:9

How can we be in the prophetic forefront of our day? How can we be the good news in a day when societies are changing dramatically all over the world? The change from agriculture to industrialization continues to occur in many emerging nations, while Europe, Japan, and North America are entering the Information Age. How can we restore equality in our day?

We need to understand our times and seasons. To restore equality, to be good news to the poor, means seeking to understand the structures of present societies. We need to understand politics, economics, and culture. As Joseph Smith, Jr., was inspired to say over 150 years ago: "And verily I say unto you that it is my will that you should hasten...to obtain a knowledge of history, and of countries, and of kingdoms, of laws of God and man, and all this for the salvation of Zion" (Doctrine and Covenants 90:12).

The restoration of equality for an enslaved, oppressed people in Egypt meant understanding their slavery, the structures of power in Egyptian society, and the God-inspired opportunities for freedom. The restoration of equality in settled agricultural Palestine meant understanding agricultural society, the importance of land, and realistic ways of maintaining equality. Do we understand our world today? Do we understand why there is hunger? Do we understand the power structures of our nation as well as of our global society? Are we able to perceive the realistic God-given opportunities before us, where God has indeed parted the sea? Until we begin to understand our world, past and present—no matter our enthusiasm for the gospel—we shall be like Don Quixote, tilting at windmills, comic but irrelevant.

We turn now to begin the attempt at better understanding our present world. The next chapter looks at some of the causes and costs of inequality. It is an incomplete and tentative beginning at seeking to understand how our discipleship can be relevant in today's world. In this exploration you are invited to bring with you a divine bias, the perspective of the poor. It is a perspective common to Moses, Jesus, and Joseph Smith, Jr. They all understood what it was like to be poor.

STUDY QUESTIONS

1. Do you think inequality is a consequence of sin, divinely ordained, or the result of some other cause?
2. In what ways has exodus been a recurring theme in the Bible?
3. Read Leviticus 25:8-34 in Today's English Version as well as in other versions.
   a. What was the Jubilee Year or Year of Restoration?
   b. How often did it occur?
   c. How was it initiated?
   d. Who actually owned the land?
4. Compare Isaiah 61:1 and 58:6 with Luke 4:18, 19. Do you feel the spirit of the Lord is upon you to be good news to the poor . . .?
5. Is it significant that Jesus did not finish reading Isaiah 61:2 in the synagogue in Nazareth? Does this point to a new way in which God would accomplish the kingdom's purpose: the way of suffering love rather than vengeance?
6. Compare Matthew 25:35, 36 (Inspired Version 25:36, 37) and Luke 4:18. Do you find parallels between the two scriptures as claimed in the text?
7. Economic equality and its restoration has been the theme of this chapter. Is this a faithful or a biased interpretation of the Bible, Christian history, and Restoration history? Give reasons for your answers.
8. Economic equality, the fruit of genuine conversion, appears to have been a continuing emphasis in the Book of Mormon, the Doctrine and Covenants, nineteenth-century Latter Day Saint

history, and in the ministry of Frederick M. Smith. However, many Latter Day Saints are now affluent westerners in a world where 80 percent of the world's population is very poor. What is the danger of losing in the last half of the twentieth century the significance of a very important Restoration distinctive?

9. Do you agree that in order to be an effective Christian disciple today, you have to understand something about economics, politics, sociology, and culture? How do you think you can begin going about this? What are some possible hazards?
10. Do you believe that God is on the side of the poor? What does that mean in today's world?

NOTES

1. J. C. Howkendijk, "Mission—A Celebration of Freedom," *Union Seminary Quarterly Review* 21, no. 2, part 1 (January 1966): 141.
2. R. North, *Sociology of the Biblical Jubilee* (Roma: Pontifico Institute Biblico, 1954), 228; and R. Sloan cited by R. Sider, *Christ and Violence* (Tring, Herts: Lion, 1980), 15.
3. A. Trocme, *Jesus and the Non-Violent Revolution,* trans. M. H. Shank and M. E. Miller (Scottdale, Pennsylvania: Herald Press, 1973), 29.
4. Ibid., 42, 43.
5. Ibid., 46, 47.
6. Ibid., 50, 51.
7. Ibid., 68.
8. Ibid., 46.
9. Compare Matthew 25:35, 36 and Luke 4:18.
10. Trocme, 70.
11. Warren Jennings, "The City in the Garden: Social Conflict in Jackson County, Missouri" in F. M. McKiernan, A. R. Blair, and P. M. Edwards, eds., *The Restoration Movement: Essays in Mormon History* (Lawrence, Kansas: Coronado Press, 1973), 101.
12. Robert Flanders, "To Transform History: Early Mormon Culture and the Concept of Time and Space," *Church History* 40, no. 1 (March 1971): 110.
13. A Book of Commandments, For the Government of the Church of Christ (Zion: W. W. Phelps, 1833) chapter XLIV:26-30.
14. L. J. Arrington, F. Y. Fox, and D. L. May, *Building the City of God: Community and Cooperation Among the Mormons* (Salt Lake City, Utah: Deseret Book Company, 1976), 15.
15. Ibid., 16.
16. Ibid., 34.
17. Ibid., 38.
18. Frederick M. Smith, *Foundations of Zion: Social Needs and Divine Purposes* (Independence, Missouri: Herald House, 1951), 69.
19. F. M. Smith, 67.
20. Ibid., 73-74.
21. Ibid., 19.

Those who have never seen the inhabitants of a nineteenth-century London slum can have no idea of the state to which dirt, drink, and economics can reduce human beings.

—Leonard Woolf[1]

To allow 40,000 children to die. . .every day is unconscionable in a world which has mastered the means of preventing it.

—James P. Grant[2]

The problem of dwindling world resources is not the result of Third World population growth—200 million U.S. citizens consume the equivalent of 10.5 billion Indians.[3]

Shall economic systems function as though all people mattered or only a few?

—Anonymous

CHAPTER 2
THE COSTS OF INEQUALITY

The State of the World's Children

From 1820 to 1945 there were at least fifty-nine million deaths from human violence.[4] The total between 1820 and the 1980s may be about seventy million. Since 1960 an average of 1,330 are killed every day.[5] This is the terrible human cost of war and violence in recent history.

In comparison fifteen million children die every year at the rate of 40,000 every day. This is equivalent to the entire under-five population of the United States or the combined young-child populations of Britain, France, Italy, Spain, and West Germany being wiped out.[6] This means in just the years between 1975 and 1985, 150 million children have perished due to entirely preventable disease and malnutrition. That exceeds, by eighty million, all those killed in war since 1820. For every person currently killed in war, thirty children die victims of poverty. Every preventable death, however caused, is a tragedy. Armed violence is a sickening feature of human life, but we have grossly underestimated the violence of economic and political systems which permit this daily slaughter of children. For every child who dies, a further six live on in poverty in stunted bodies with stunted minds.[7]

> No statistic can express what it is to see even one child die in such a way; to see a mother sitting hour after anxious hour leaning her child's body against her own; to see the child's head turn on limbs which are unnaturally still, stiller than in sleep; to want to stop even that small movement because it is so obvious that there is so little energy left inside the child's life; to see the living pink at the roof of the child's mouth in shocking contrast to the

already dead-looking greyness of the skin, the colors of its life and death; to see the uncomprehending panic in eyes which are still the clear and lucid eyes of a child; and then to know, in one endless moment, that life has gone.[8]

In the 1840s Thomas Carlyle wrote, "England is full of wealth, of multifarious produce, supply for human want of every kind. Yet England is dying."[9] What could not be hidden from Carlyle nearly 150 years ago—that there is enough and to spare for all—is far more obvious today. A UNICEF report maintains that "to allow 40,000 children to die like this every day is unconscionable in a world which has mastered the means of preventing it."[10]

But why do 40,000 children a day, one every two seconds, perish? To understand better we have to know something of the historical development of the world's economy and how it is working today.

Some History

The present world economy has a history which begins as a European story.

European history had reached a take-off point in 1492, the year Columbus discovered America. It was the beginning of a new age and of many changes in European society. Technological progress was accelerating. The printing press had been invented. So had the gun. The following hundred years saw the Reformation, the development of the nation-state, and the beginnings of nationalism. The feudal economy was breaking down as capitalism was being born.

In all this, however, it would be a mistake to suppose that European civilization was the most advanced in the world. It was not. China, India, Japan, Central and South America, and West Africa all contained flourishing civilizations. The only lead Europe had initially, perhaps, was in the making of guns. Europe was at the beginning of its empires. In 1492, only 9 percent of the world was controlled by Europeans. By 1935, 85 percent of the land area and 70 percent of the world's population were controlled by Europeans.[11]

The Spanish and Portuguese in their quest for gold destroyed the civilizations of Central and South America, inflicting great suffering on the native peoples. Conversion to Christianity at the point of the sword completed their conquest. Northern Europeans invaded and colonized North America. At first there was peace between native Americans and Europeans, then the Europeans broke treaty after treaty. By the end of the nineteenth century, the Indians of North America were virtually prisoners in their own land.

To work the plantations of the European settlers in the Americas, slave labor was imported from Africa resulting in the destruction of West African civilization and enormous human suffering. In Australia and New Zealand history repeated itself in the treatment of the aboriginal peoples; the natives of Tasmania were completely exterminated.

It was as much by force of arms and violence as by trade and investment that Europeans gained control of most of the world. With the invention of the machine gun, Europeans ruled the world by the end of the nineteenth century.

Capitalism—private ownership and production for a market—was a European invention. Its development caused enormous human suffering in England among the poor, but at the same time created great wealth for a few. The commercialization of agriculture, especially in the growing of sheep for wool in England, led to the enclosure movement. Rich farmers and landowners took the common land, which before had belonged to everyone, and made it their private property. The poor—cheated of their common land rights—became beggars or worked for low wages in the newly developing factories.

This pattern of making communal land private property was repeated by the British everywhere they went—India, Africa, and elsewhere. Landless peasants in British colonies were forced to work on plantations or starve.

Cottage industries of weaving and spinning, carried out by families, were wiped out in England by the Industrial Revolution. Everywhere the British Empire extended—India, Egypt, Africa—the local cottage industries were wiped out, and sometimes, in the early days, not just by competition. Indian textiles, for instance, were cheaper than English textiles initially. In consequence Bengali weavers were forbidden by law to weave. If they did their hands were cut off. As Lord Brentford stated, "We did not conquer India for the benefit of the Indians. We conquered India as an outlet for the goods of Great Britain. We conquered India by the sword and by the sword we should hold it."[12]

It has been argued that the rapid development of Europe was accompanied by the underdevelopment of the colonies. The poor and vulnerable at home and abroad were sacrificed in this process. Unrestrained capitalism widened the gap between rich and poor within a nation, while imperialism created greater inequality between nations.

As the nation-state developed in Europe, and as the respective commercial empires grew, conflict arose.

Their nationalism and competition for markets resulted in two terrible world wars in this century.

In the nineteenth century, beginning with Robert Owen, socialist movements in Europe developed in response to capitalism. The most infamous kind of socialism was that developed by Marx and Engels who brilliantly and passionately analyzed Victorian capitalism. Marx, although more internationally minded than most Europeans, was very much a European. And although Marxist theories are claimed to be universal, they are in fact limited by his European perspectives. He never questioned Europe's patriarchal culture or industrialization. His view of nature was the same as the capitalists he criticized (nature was to be conquered, not lived with in harmony). Finally, the violence inherent in European culture found expression in Marxist class conflict and the Russian Revolution. Industrialization of Soviet Russia under Stalin was as tragic and cruel as industrialization had been in England.

Ironically, although he did most of his work in England, Marx was virtually ignored by British nineteenth-century socialists. The legacy of Owenism, which includes the cooperative movement, trade unionism, and the extension of voting rights to working people, enabled the twentieth-century development of social democracy—socialists acquiring power and reform constitutionally and thus peacefully.

The Modern World Economy

The Keynesian Revolution

The capitalist economy—while creating unprecedented wealth—first inflicted human suffering by a ruthless competition which enriched a few and pauperized many. Second, it inflicted tremendous suffering by the uncontrollable business cycles of booms and slumps. It was in the middle of the devastating 1930s that British economist Milton Keynes produced his general theory on the business cycle. Keynes said that the booms and slumps of the business cycle could be controlled by governments spending more money in a slump and less in a boom. His theory seemed to be validated by the experience of the New Deal in the United States, and especially so in World War II when American living standards rose, full employment existed, and the economy expanded even while fighting a world war.

After the war Keynesian economics helped Western governments reform capitalism by controlling the booms and slumps of the business cycle, thereby eliminating much human suffering, and by increasing spending on health, social security, and education in the development of the welfare state so that all citizens, rich or poor, young or old, had their needs met.

International agreement, led by the United States, after the war enabled international trade to expand rapidly. The United States practiced global Keynesianism by investing money in Europe and Japan, thus preventing a slump in its own economy while enabling the war-devastated economies of Europe and Japan to rebuild.

Keynesian economics had one problem—it could not easily control inflation in the 1970s. It was in this decade that the Keynesian era ended. The Vietnam War and the oil crisis created high inflation. The political climate changed, with a return in Britain and the United States to encouraging old-fashioned capitalism. Keynesian economics were abandoned and monetarist economic policies adopted. These policies, especially those of the United States, helped produce—at the beginning of the 1980s—the worst slump or recession since the 1930s. Inflation had been controlled. People's savings and wealth were perhaps safer, but at the cost of millions of unemployed and much suffering—especially in the Third World. To these costs we shall return, but now it is important to understand the organization of the global economy after World War II.

Organization of the Global Economy

In 1944 at Bretton Woods, New Hampshire, under the leadership of the United States, forty-four nations met to organize a strategy for economic recovery after the Second World War. Two institutions were born: The World Bank and the International Monetary Fund (IMF). The World Bank was originally established to help Europe and Japan rebuild their war-devastated economies. Today it is a major source of loans and development expertise for Third World nations. The IMF was originally organized to help nations with short-term, balance of payments problems. Today it has grown in influence and power to become almost a central bank for the world economy. Another institution was added shortly after the conference—the General Agreement on Tariffs and Trade (GATT). GATT's objectives, then and now, are to liberalize world trade by reducing tariffs. All three institutions work together; to belong to one, a nation has to be subject to the other two.

The strategy for economic recovery initiated at Bretton Woods, together with the implementation of Keynesian policies by national governments, has appeared to be successful for expanding trade and economic growth.

However, not all have been undisputed winners in this developing economy. The global economy is first of all dominated by the rich industrialized countries and tends to operate in the interests of the already affluent nations. For instance, it is easy for Third World nations to export raw materials and agricultural goods to richer nations, but processed food and manufactured goods are charged high tariffs to enter the markets of most industrialized countries. In the recent recession, rising protectionism has further hindered the lot of Third World exports. Thus GATT is not always uniformly fair.

The IMF is controlled by directors who represent nations according to their economic power:

> As the nation with the largest economy, the U.S. wields approximately 20 percent of the voting strength. The ten richest developed countries control more than 50 percent of the voting power. Thirty-seven low income African countries on the other hand. . .have a cumulative vote of less than 6 percent of the IMF's total.[13]

The IMF has enormous power, not only through its own lending, but also because of the IMF-imposed economic policies for approval of loans from other sources. The cost of IMF-imposed economic policies falls particularly hard on the poor and results in increased human suffering and a widening gap between rich and poor.

The World Bank's activities have shown some tragic results borne by the poor, despite what appear to be genuine attempts to be helpful.

UNICEF has summarized the world situation today:

The industrialized nations, containing a quarter of the world's people, still control more than three quarters of the world's wealth. By and large, that gives them the power to lay down the rules of world trade, regulate the workings of the international monetary system, decide what investments will be made and where, determine the course of scientific and technological research, and organize the international division of labor largely in their own interests. As a result, the majority of developing countries have correspondingly little control over the price they receive for the raw materials they have to sell, or the price they pay for the manufactured goods they have to buy, or the value of the currency they must use, or the world monetary system within which they must earn their living, or the terms of the investments they seek, or the amounts and conditions of the aid they receive.[14]

The Impact of the World's Economy on the Poor

Since the Second World War most of the colonized nations have achieved political independence. However, economic independence is another matter. As has already been pointed out, the developed nations led by the United States still control the world's economic institutions—largely to their benefit.

The economics of the developing nations, distorted during the process of colonization, often are still limited to plantation crops for export to developed nations. Such crops suffer unattainable prices and sometimes, as in the case of sisal in Tanzania, decline in real terms against the value of manufactured goods.[15] With the best land frequently used in the Third World for export crops, food production for local consumption is often confined to marginal land. Meanwhile the Third World astonishingly exports more agricultural products to the developed nations, including the United States, than is imported or given as aid.[16] So while we, as affluent consumers in rich nations, enjoy coffee, peanuts, beef, bananas, and roses, substantial numbers of the poorest of the poor go hungry in many Third World countries.

The problem of hunger in the world is caused by poverty, *not* the lack of available food. There is indeed "enough and to spare," and except for Africa, per capita food production has continued to increase worldwide.[17] If there is a population problem, it is because there is a poverty problem. There is an unfair distribution of wealth.

The result today is that 25 percent of the world's population consumes 80 percent of the world's income. The wealth of the rich nations, measured by GNP, is on average 6 times greater than for Costa Rica, 40 times Tanzania, 56 times India, and 107 times Bangladesh.[18] As a consequence average life expectancy in the Third World, except for China, is 48 years compared with 74 years in the United States.[19]

The gap between rich and poor nations continues to grow. The real growth in wealth per capita between 1960 and 1982 was 3.1 percent for poor countries and 3.4 percent for rich countries.[20] "When you rip aside the confusing figures on growth rates, you find that for almost two-thirds of humanity the increase in income has been less than $1 a year for the last twenty years."[21]

One of the most important developments since the Second World War has been the development of an interdependent world economy. "The revolutionary development of technology in transportation and communication has made markets in different countries interdependent to an ever larger extent than previously."[22] The result has been that all but the poorest developing countries have been increasingly integrated into the world market economy. Two indications of this interdependence have been the current debt crisis and the most recent recession.

As has already been mentioned in the discussion of Keynesian economics, it appeared that from the end of the Second World War until the end of the 1970s the business cycle of individual national economies was manageable. However, at the beginning of the 1980s—with changes in economic policies in the United States and other industrialized nations—the world entered a recession second only to that of the 1930s. In an increasingly integrated world economy what has been the impact of the recession on the world's poor? In the 1984 State of the World's Children Report, UNICEF stated the conclusions of ten economists:

> In all countries, the poor spend a greater proportion of their incomes on necessities such as food or fuel or basic medical care. Any decline in that income therefore threatens not just material progress but the ability to maintain health and life. In such circumstances, the risk is greatest to the growing minds and bodies of young children.
>
> This economic vulnerability is paralleled by the political vulnerability of the poor. Many of the mechanisms which link the international economic system to the poor neighborhoods of the developing world are mechanisms which act like reverse shock absorbers—increasing the impact of recession as they pass that impact down the line. It has been estimated, for example, that a 1 percent fall in the rate of growth of the industrialized countries tends to produce a 1.5 percent fall in the average rate of growth of the developing countries. Within the developing nations themselves, an echo of that same process passes the economic shockwave on to the poorest sections of their own societies. A 2 percent to 3 percent decline in the average income of a developing nation, for example, can easily result in a 10 percent to 15 percent decline in the income of the poorest classes. Finally, this same process may happen again within the poor communities themselves; in many societies, females and young children

depend on what is left—of the evening meal and of the weekly wage—after their husbands and older sons and brothers have met their needs.

By such mechanisms is the greatest burden of the world economic recession passed on to those who are least able to sustain it. Ironically, the main protection for the very poor has been the fact that so many of them live in rural areas which are only peripherally linked to the world economy. Although many of the rural poor have escaped the full impact of the recession, drought and poor harvests have had a serious effect, particularly in the last two years.[23]

Hopes that capitalism had been effectively reformed have now vanished with the failure of Keynesian economics. In our global market economy, the poor—especially women and children—are victimized as cruelly as ever. Yet the relationship of rich nations with poor nations does not have to continue to be a win-lose situation:

It was a major conclusion of the Interfuture Study of 1979 that the longer-run prospects for the industrialized countries are substantially better in scenarios in which the developing countries progress harmoniously and that it is in the interest of developed countries to co-operate with and support such progress.[24]

Unfortunately we live in a time of militant conservatism and nationalism in the majority of rich nations, with no global vision or much compassion for even the poor at home. For instance, in the most recent recession the poor in the United States have also suffered in increasing numbers: "In the four years between 1979 and 1983, the number of those living in poverty increased by over nine million people. During this same period, the number of poor children under the age of six jumped by 51 percent."[25] Again, it is little children who pay the costs of adjustments in our world economy. The impact of the world economy is most cruel on the vulnerable—the poor and the children of the poor.

What About Development Aid?

In light of these inequalities between rich and poor nations, how effective is development aid? Overseas Development Aid (ODA) as a percentage of GNP is shown below.

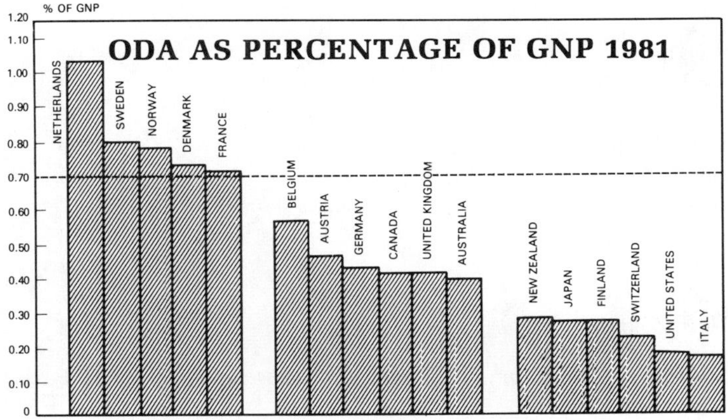

Source: OECD Press Release, 1982
Development Cooperation 1981 Review (OECD, Paris, 1981)

As can be seen, Britain (the greatest former imperalist) and the United States (the world's greatest economy and inventor of foreign aid) are currently among the lowest aid givers, falling far short of the 0.70 percent of GNP given as a target by the United Nations.

Some idea of dollar amounts given every month per person in rich nations is shown in Table 2.1, on the next page. It is minimal in real terms. Private giving through churches and other organizations is the equivalent of a hamburger given by a United States citizen once a month.

Table 2:1
AID TO THIRD WORLD COUNTRIES 1983

	Government Aid per citizen per month (U.S. $)	Private Aid per person per month (U.S. $)
Sweden	7.55	0.61
Netherlands	6.99	0.62
France	5.89	0.05
West Germany	4.29	0.50
Canada	4.89	0.44
Australia	4.20	0.17
United Kingdom	2.38	0.12
Japan	2.66	0.02
U.S.A.	2.88	0.47
New Zealand	1.60	0.18

Source: 1. *Development Cooperation 1984 Review* (OECD, Paris, 1984)
2. Population figures used in calculations *OECD Observer*, 1983

Thus foreign aid at present levels and under present conditions is woefully insufficient to compensate Third World nations for unjust economic systems and inadequate to enable real development to occur.

The Necessity of Equality

To abolish hunger means the elimination of poverty. To eliminate poverty means to move toward equality, to recognize the unique worth of all humans, and to devise economies which function as though people mattered. Some national economies, despite low levels of wealth, have achieved remarkable results: China, Taiwan, Korea, Sri Lanka, and Costa Rica. Land reform in Japan, Korea, and Taiwan has aided development and bettered conditions for large numbers of citizens. The world already has economies in the Third World which function as though people mattered.

In Europe, North America, and elsewhere, the excesses of Victorian capitalism were increasingly curbed by moral indignation and the pressure of the poor for a democratic vote, and thus, a say in the economy. It culminated in the welfare states of industrialized Western nations. As societies recognized the equality of all adults in politics, so they had to respond in economics. Where political systems were unable to adapt peacefully, revolution often resulted.

Unfortunately, the vast majority of the world's poor are excluded from any sense of political equality. Governments in the Third World are often a form of dictatorship—frequently supported by the United States or the USSR. Furthermore, the poor in the Third World have no say in how the world's economy functions or how the world's wealth is shared. The political leaders of the United States are arguably the most influential leaders of the world. The United States economy represents 25 percent of the world's wealth. Indirectly, even today, the United States exerts a vast influence in shaping the world's affairs, as has already been pointed out.

To some extent the poor can hold the rich accountable in democratic countries. However, worldwide there is no political mechanism whereby the poor of the earth can hold the affluent accountable. That is why they suffer so much. Democracy—which is an expression of the equal worth of persons—simply has not been extended far enough. It has to be extended politically and then result in economic change. If it should be extended peacefully then there would be peaceful changes toward equality. If the voice of the poor is not heard, then revolution cannot be ruled out. The poor increasingly have nothing to lose except their poverty. The economist, Barbara Ward, wrote:

> The vastly outnumbered quarter of humanity who live in reasonable affluence are, on the whole, inward-looking in both their interests and their aims. But so were the courtiers of Versailles and the bureaucratic elite of czarist Russia. If wisdom, good will, and vision are insufficient to awaken the sense of need for new directions, there are more violent and ominous routes. As the twentieth century moves to its last decades, its day-to-day experience—from Belfast to Mogadishu, from Amsterdam to Bulawayo—is very far from suggesting that violence, terrorism, even a sort of fusing of local and planetary civil war are lethal possibilities that can be comfortably ruled out. A billion earthlings now live in unspeakable misery. Another billion are on the way. Can their passivity and patience be made the safe foundation for greedy minorities either at home or in the planet itself? This is not what history has to teach. Nor is there much time in which to learn.[26]

It is those of us who vote, spend, and worship in the world's industrial democracies who could be the prophetic voice for change from within the bastions of power. By our citizenship and financial stewardship we can amplify the prophetic message being shouted by the world's poor. Together—through organizations like Bread for the World in the United States and the World Development Movement in Britain—we can make a difference. In whatever we do, however, change is inevitable.

STUDY QUESTIONS

1. Read the following modern parable:

   A traveler, driving down an unfamiliar highway, encountered a treacherous place in the roadway. An unmarked curve in the road, next to a steep embankment, resulted in a demolished car and injury to the unfortunate traveler. A motorist, traveling not far behind, passed on by, having seen the accident, but wanting to believe there was nothing he could do to help. A second motorist came by but, not wanting to get involved, went on his way as well. But a certain devout Christian, who lived in that neighborhood, also saw the accident. She knew what must be done, as numerous other travelers had previously suffered a similar misfortune at this same treacherous curve. She called an ambulance, saw the traveler safely to the local hospital, assisted in disposition of the wrecked automobile, and aided the unfortunate traveler in every possible way as she had helped others before.

   The traveler, when sufficiently recovered, asked why the treacherous curve had not been straightened, or at least a warning sign erected. The devout Christian answered that the curve had been there for many years, that no one had ever seriously proposed straightening it, and that the adjoining land belonged to a wealthy landowner who would no doubt oppose any change in the roadway. And besides, she took some pride (righteous pride of course) in her willingness to generously assist any who had such misfortune on the curve. Perplexed and somewhat surprised, the traveler pondered this answer as he lay in the hospital bed.[27]

   a. What would be the more effective ministry for this devout Christian—continue to rescue the victims of the treacherous curve or work to get the curve straightened?
   b. How can this parable be applied to economic and political systems? What are its implications?

c. Should the church's ministry be rescuing the victims of society or changing society to reduce the number of victims?

2. Moves toward economic equality are highly controversial. What is said about economic equality by
   a. our culture,
   b. the Judeo-Christian tradition, and
   c. the Restoration movement?

   Is there a tension between what our culture may be telling us and what our religious traditions say?
3. Children, it is pointed out, suffer the most in our global economy, both at home and abroad. Why do you think this is so? Is it right?
4. Are you convinced that there are more than enough resources, when shared equitably, to adequately feed, house, clothe, and protect medically all the world's people?
5. Are the poor largely responsible for their condition or are they victims of history and economic and political systems over which they have little or no control?
6. Table 2.1, page 54, shows monthly giving through taxation and through private charitable organizations to the Third World. Is it surprising to find giving to Third World countries so low?
7. How could you influence your nation's government to benefit more the poor at home and abroad? What organizations do you know who could help you?

NOTES

1. Leonard Woolf, "Sowing" (1960), cited in George Dalton, *Economic Systems and Society: Capitalism, Communism and the Third World* (Middlesex: Penguin, 1979), 66.
2. James P. Grant, *The State of the World's Children, 1982-83* (New York: UNICEF), 1.
3. Sue Carroll, et. al, "Organizing for Social Transformation" in C. R. Beitz and T. Herman, eds., *Peace and War* (San Francisco: W. H. Freeman and Co., 1973), 424.
4. Richardson (1960), cited by Peter A. Corning, "Human Violence: Some Causes and Implications" in Beitz and Herman, 119.
5. *New Internationalist* (March 1983): 10-11.
6. James P. Grant, *The State of the World's Children,* 1984 (New York: UNICEF), 4.
7. Grant, 1982-83, 1.
8. Ibid.
9. Cited by Jeremy Seabrook, "Why the Rich Need the Poor," *The Guardian* 29 (July 1985): 9.
10. Grant, 1982-83, 1.
11. Alvin Toffler, *The Third Wave* (New York: Bantam Books, 1981), 91.
12. Lord Brentford (1930) cited by William L. Shirer in *Gandhi—A Memoir* (London: Abacus, 1981), frontispiece.
13. *Outreach on Hunger Resource Materials* (Washington, D.C.: Bread for the World Educational Fund, 1985), 126-127.
14. Grant, 1984, 36.
15. "Crop Prices Fall," *New Internationalist* (July 1982): 5. Also "Black Africa: In Shambles," *Newsweek* (July 19, 1982, Asia Edition): 28.
16. See *U.N. Handbook of International Trade and Development Statistics,* 1972 and 1980.
17. See *EAO Production Year Book,* 1980 and later.
18. Calculated from figures found in *Development Cooperation 1982 Review* (Paris: OECD, 1982).
19. *Pastoral Letter on Social Teachings and the U.S. Economy,* Outline First Draft, National Conference of Catholic Bishops, Washington, D.C.; *National Catholic Reporter* (November 23, 1984): 25, paragraph 274.

20. *Outreach on Hunger Resource Materials,* Table El, 90.
21. Mahbub ul Hag, cited in *Outreach on Hunger Resource Materials,* 19.
22. *World Economic Interdependence and the Evolving North-South Relationship* (Paris: OECD, 1983), 9.
23. Grant, 1984, 37.
24. *World Economic Interdependence,* 10.
25. *Pastoral Letter,* 22, paragraph 187.
26. Barbara Ward, *Progress for a Small Planet* (New York: W. W. Norton & Company, 1979), 170.
27. D. G. Graham, "An Ethical Perspective on World Hunger and Public Policy," Maurice L. Draper, ed., *Restoration Studies II* (Independence, Missouri: Herald House, 1983), 37-38.

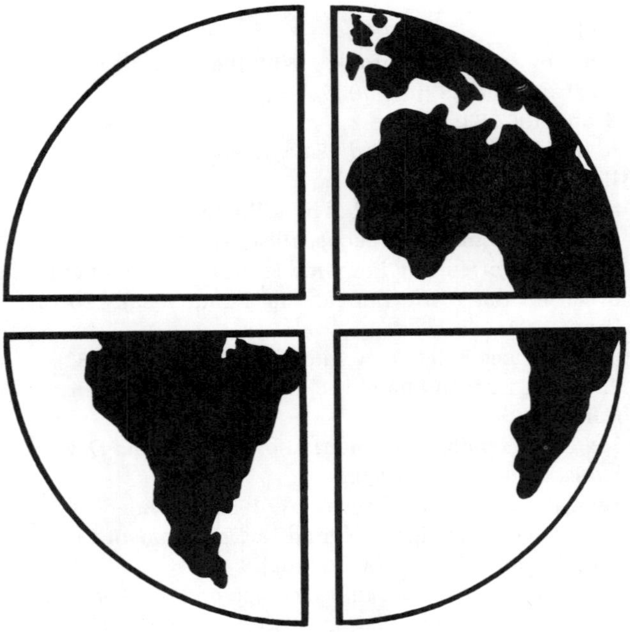

It is the New Testament witness that God's answer to evil in this world lies in the cross.

—John Ferguson[1]

To be sure, [Jesus] did not say that one should practice loving non-violence because it would always instantly transform economics into bosom friends. The cross stands as a harsh reminder that love for enemies does not always work—at least in the short run.

—Ronald Sider[2]

Though I cannot claim to be a Christian in the sectarian sense, the example of Jesus' suffering is a factor in the composition of my undying faith in non-violence which rules all my actions, worldly and temporal. . . . Jesus lived and died in vain if he did not teach us to regulate the whole of life by the eternal law of love.

—M. K. Gandhi[3]

The sign of the nuclear age is the Bomb. The sign of Christ is the Cross. The Bomb is the countersign to the Cross; it arrogantly threatens to undo the work that the Cross has done. In the Cross all things are reconciled; in the Bomb, all things are destroyed. In the Cross violence is defeated; in the Bomb, violence is victorious. In the Cross, evil has been overcome; in the Bomb, evil has dominion. In the Cross, death is swallowed up; in the Bomb death reigns supreme. Which will hold sway in our times?

—Jim Wallis[4]

CHAPTER 3
RESTORING PEACE—THE CHRISTIAN TRADITIONS

Jesus, Peace, and the Cross

The angels who witnessed the birth of Jesus sang, "On earth peace among men" (Luke 2:14 RSV). Yet the world Jesus was born into was far from peaceful. Martin Hengel describes it thus:

> For the unsophisticated Jewish population, it was almost entirely a history of oppressive exploitation, wars of indescribable brutality and disappointed hopes. The rule of Herod and his sons and the corrupt regime of the procurators—Pilate not least among them—had made the situation in Jewish Palestine so intolerable that apparently only three possibilities remained: armed revolutionary resistance, more or less opportunistic accommodations to the establishment—leaving open the possibility of mental reservations—and patient passive endurance.[5]

Into such a world Jesus was to demonstrate another way—"the way of suffering servanthood and unconditional love for enemies grounded in God's unmerited mercy towards sinners."[6]

The temptation to achieve the kingdom of God by violence was nevertheless a very real option for Jesus. We see it in the second temptation (Luke 4:5-8) in which Satan offers Jesus all the kingdoms of the world if Jesus would only give homage to him. Jesus resists the temptation to use the methods of Satan to achieve the kingdom of God. After one more testing Satan departs, biding his time for future opportunities.

Satan's time was to come again when Peter recognized at Caesarea Philippi that Jesus is the Christ (Matthew 16:14-26; Mark 8:28-38). Jesus responded to Peter's inspired insight by stating publicly his anticipation of cross and suffering. Peter's opposition to this was rebuked by Jesus as a further temptation of Satan.

In the incident where John and James wanted to call down fire as Elijah did—on an unwelcoming Samaritan village—Jesus rebuked them (Luke 9:52-56). Commenting on this incident, G. B. Caird has stated:

> James and John wanted to emulate Elijah (II Kings 1:9-16); but we must recognize that in this respect Elijah was typical of the whole Old Testament, which knew no other way of dealing with enemies of Israel than to call down God's curse upon them. This is why Elijah had to disappear from the mountain to give place to Jesus, with his new way of loving his enemies and dying for them, and to the new conception of God which that way implied.[7]

Jesus, in his entry into Jerusalem on a donkey, is described as the fulfillment of Zechariah 9:9 which depicts the Messiah coming, not on a warrior's horse, but humble, mounted on an ass. Zechariah continues, "I will cut off the chariot from E'phraim and the war horse from Jerusalem; and the battle bow shall be cut off, and he shall command peace to the nations; his dominion shall be from sea to sea, and from the River to the ends of the earth" (Zechariah 9:10 RSV). Jesus was thus symbolizing a "new Messiah, standing not for war and military victory but for disarmament and peace."[8]

Jesus' struggle in Gethsemane was the struggle between choosing the cup of violence and the cup of suffering love—the cross as the method to redeem his people. The intensity of the struggle for Jesus is vividly described in the gospel passages. The conclusion Jesus finally reached is clearly indicated at his arrest, when one of his disciples drew a sword in defense of Jesus and injured a servant of the High Priest. Jesus' reaction is stunningly clear: "Put your sword back into its place; for all who take the sword will perish by the sword" (Matthew 26:52 RSV). In commenting on this moment the early church Father, Tertullian, declared that Jesus "cursed the works of the sword for ever after."[9]

The cross then—the choice of Jesus—is God's ultimate argument against violence. Love is the ultimate method of bringing us to peace. The cross is the ultimate demonstration of how God deals with enemies—through suffering love. The word of grace is backed by costly self-giving on the cross.

The teaching of Jesus in the Sermon on the Mount should be seen in the light of his subsequent suffering on the cross. In Jesus God loved his enemies. Thus with an authority that exceeds Moses, Jesus could say:

> You have heard that it was said, "An eye for an eye and a tooth for a tooth," But I say to you, Do not resist one who is evil. But if any one strikes you on the right cheek, turn to him the other also; and if any one would sue you and take your coat, let him have your cloak as well; and if any one forces you to go one mile, go with him two miles. Give to him who begs from you, and do not refuse him who would borrow from you. You have heard that it was said, "You shall love your neighbor and hate your enemy." But I say to you, Love your enemies and pray for those who persecute you, so that you may be sons of your Father who is in heaven; for he makes his sun rise on the evil and on the good, and sends rain on the just and on the unjust. For if you love those who love you, what reward have you? Do not even the tax collectors do the same? And if you salute only your brethren, what more are you doing than others? Do not even the Gentiles do the same? You, therefore, must be perfect, as your heavenly Father is perfect.—Matthew 5:38-48 RSV

Only by extending the same grace to others,

granted by God freely to each of us, can we become peacemakers and be blessed.

It helps to remember that the gospel of Matthew was probably written some fifty years or more after the crucifixion. It is the epistles of Paul, written a generation before Matthew and Luke, that are the earliest written accounts of the Christian tradition. In Romans, Paul writes:

Bless those who persecute you; bless and do not curse them. . . . Repay no one evil for evil, but take thought for what is noble in the sight of all. If possible, so far as it depends upon you, live peaceably with all. Beloved, never avenge yourselves, but leave it to the wrath of God; for it is written, "Vengeance is mine, I will repay, says the Lord." No, "if your enemy is hungry, feed him; if he is thirsty, give him drink; for by so doing you will heap burning coals upon his head." Do not be overcome by evil, but overcome evil with good.—Romans 12:14, 17-21 RSV

Thus, both Paul and the writer of Matthew's gospel witness to the same central tradition of peacemaking in the first-century church. Yet this is not all, for we see the same tradition reappearing in I Peter, which was written either at the end of the first century or the beginning of the second.

Do not return evil for evil or reviling for reviling; but on the contrary bless, for to this you have been called, that you may obtain a blessing. . . . And keep your conscience clear, so that, when you are abused, those who revile your good behavior in Christ may be put to shame. For it is better to suffer for doing right, if that should be God's will, than for doing wrong. For Christ also died for sins once for all, the righteous for the unrighteous, that he might bring us to God, being put to death in the flesh but made alive in the spirit.—I Peter 3:9, 16-18 RSV

If there is anything certain in the New Testament witness it is this: God treats us wonderfully better than we deserve and whatever the merits or evilness of others, God expects his disciples to treat others with equal kindness.

German theologian Jurgen Moltmann has stated:

Everything that can be categorized as "non-violence" in the sayings and actions of Jesus can ultimately be derived from this "revolution in the concept of God" which he set forth: namely, that God comes not to carry out just revenge upon the evil, but to justify sinners by grace, whether they are Zealots or tax collectors, Pharisees or sinners.[10]

In agreement Ronald Sider wrote, "Jesus' vicarious cross for sinners is the foundation and deepest expression of Jesus' command to love one's enemies."[11]

One can conclude that there is clear consistency about how the first-century Christians understood the teachings of Jesus on peace. We now turn to the second- and third-century church to see the remarkable continuity in this peaceable tradition.

The Pacificism of the Church in the Second and Third Centuries

It is clear that the Christian church in the second and third centuries was pacifistic. This is documented by the following early Christian writers:[12]

Justin Martyr (killed A.D. 165)

You can be convinced that this has happened. . . . We who used to kill one another, do not make war on our enemies. We refuse to tell lies or deceive our inquisitors; we prefer to die acknowledging Christ.—I *Apology*, 39

We who were filled with war and mutual slaughter and all wickedness have each and all throughout the earth changed our instruments of war, our swords into plowshares and our spears into farming-tools, and cultivate piety, justice, love of mankind, faith and the hope which we have from the Father through the Crucified one.—*The Dialogue with Trypho*, 110

Tatian (c. 160)

I do not want to be an emperor; I do not want wealth; I refuse military office; I loathe sexual looseness.—*Discourse to the Greeks*, 11

Athenagoras (c. 177)

We, thinking that to watch a man being killed is practically equivalent to taking life, refuse to attend the gladiatorial displays.—*An Embassy about the Christians,* 35

Irenaeus

If the law of liberty, that is, the Word of God, proclaimed to the whole earth by the apostles who went out from Jerusalem, has achieved a revolution of such magnitude that the very peoples have made their warlike lances and swords into plows and changed them into sickles which he gave for reaping corn, and now do not know how to fight, but when struck offer even the other cheek, the prophets made this declaration of no-one but him who accomplished it.—*Against Heresies,* 4, 56, 4

Clement of Alexandria

We are being educated not in war but in peace.—*The Tutor* 1, 12, 98

We are the race given over to peace.—*The Tutor* 2, 21, 32

We have made use of only one instrument, the peaceful word, with which we do honor to God.—*The Tutor* 4, 42

Origen (185-254)

To those who ask us where we have come from or who is our commander, we say that we have come in accordance with the counsels of Jesus to cut down our warlike and arrogant swords of dispute into plowshares, and we convert into sickles the spears we formerly used in fighting. For we no longer take sword against a nation, nor do we learn any more to make war, having become sons of peace for the sake of Jesus, who is our commander.—*Against Celsus* 5, 33

Tertullian (c. 160-222)

How shall the Christian wage war, no, how shall he even be a soldier in peace-time, without the sword which the Lord has taken away? For although soldiers had come to John and received the form of their rule, although even a centurion had believed, the Lord afterwards in disarming Peter, ungirded every soldier.—*On Idolatry,* 19

Who shall produce truth, gentleness and justice with the sword, and not their contrary deceit, harshness and injustice, which are the proper business of battles?—*Against Marcion* 3, 14

Cyprian (Bishop of Carthage 248-258)

The whole world is wet with mutual blood; and murder, which in the case of an individual is admitted to be a crime, is called a virtue when it is committed communally. Impunity is claimed for the wicked deeds, not on the plea that they are guiltless, but because cruelty is perpetrated on a grand scale.—*Letter* 1, 6

In view of this position, what would happen when a soldier was converted? The solution was a compromise. Many served in the army but never saw battle, engaging instead in construction work and other behind-the-lines tasks. The church did not demand that converts leave the army, but full church membership was not granted until they did. This is documented for instance by the following:[13]

They shall not receive into the church one of the emperor's soldiers. If they have received him he shall refuse to kill if commanded to do so. If he does not refrain he shall be rejected.—Egypt Fourth Century, Statute 28

But if soldiers wish to be baptized to the Lord, let them cease from military service or from position of authority, or else let them not be accepted.—Syrian Document, "The Testament of our Lord"

Some Christians in the tensions caused by the emperor Diocletian at the end of the third century chose to leave the army because of their convictions and suffered certain martyrdom. Some of their statements at their trials have been preserved:[14]

Because I was a Christian I have now chosen to be a civilian.—Tarachus

I threw down my arms; it was not seemly that a Christian man, who renders military service to the Lord Jesus Christ, should render it by earthly injuries.—Marcellus

I cannot serve as a soldier; I cannot do evil; I am a Christian.—Maximillian

In summarizing the first three centuries of Christian history it is clear that few Christians were soldiers and the church's teachings were pacifistic. Soon, however, the situation changed. The fourth century was a watershed period in Christian history.

Constantine and After

Beginning in the fourth century, with the actions of the emperor Constantine, a decisive change occurred in Christian history. Constantine embraced Christianity. Christians quickly moved from being a despised and persecuted minority into being members of the official religion of the Roman Empire. In that transmutation, Christian pacifism was compromised or lost. At the beginning of the fourth century the emperor Diocletian had purged the army of Christians. At the end of that century Theodosius purged the army of non-Christians. James Douglas describes Constantine's impact:

> When Constantine raised the cross above his troops, he raised before the Christian Church the same temptation which Satan had set before Christ on the mountain with the sight of all the kingdoms of the world. And the Christian Church—for understandable reasons and without the critical perspective of 1600 years—accepted Constantine's offer.[15]

In the fourth and fifth centuries, the teachings of Ambrose, bishop of Milan, and later Augustine of Hippo, saw the development of the just war theory, i.e. the conditions under which it was justified to go to war. Augustine gave guidelines for waging a just war which have been summarized as follows: (1) The intention must be to restore peace, (2) Only a legitimate authority may declare war, (3) The conduct of war must be just, (4) Monks and clerics must not engage in warfare.[16] The just war theory was originally developed by the Greeks. Ambrose and Augustine were attempting to make it Christian.

Unfortunately the principles of just war were frequently ignored in European history. In the Crusades against the Muslims—initiated and supported by the church—the principles of just war were completely abandoned.

However, the just war theory continued to receive attention. St. Thomas Aquinas—the greatest thinker of the medieval age—argued the following case for a just war: "(1) It must be waged by a public authority for the common good; (2) A just cause is required; (3) It must be fought with right intentions; and (4) The principle of proportionality 'the harm done by war must not exceed the good that comes from it.'"[17]

Luther continued in the "just war" tradition. He argued that the state might enter reluctantly into a just war, but that the only weapon of the church was the Word of God. Calvin was more aggressive. The Puritans of New England were strongly influenced by this Calvinistic tradition and thus, indirectly, may have considerably influenced not only American culture but the Restoration movement as well. Also, during the Protestant Reformation the Quakers, Anabaptists, and Brethren churches emerged as pacifistic movements.

With the rise of strong centralized nation-states and with religion largely subject to the state in Europe, it was increasingly difficult for Christian churches to lessen the evils of war. The "just war" theory has been vulnerable to misuse by the forces of nationalism. In European wars, it has been invoked by both sides down to the world wars of the twentieth century.

This rather simplistic outline is the history of the two Christian peace traditions. First, there is the pacifistic tradition that dominated Christian thought and practice from the days of Jesus up to the end of the third century. Then, after the emperor Constantine became Christian, and with the development of Christianity as the official religion of the Empire, the just war tradition developed and became dominant. For subsequent Christian history the just war theory has been the majority Christian position on war and peace.

Peace Traditions in the Restoration Movement

The Restoration church traditionally has not been one of the peace churches—such as the Quakers, the Anabaptists, and their Mennonite and Hutterite descendants.

In the Book of Mormon both the just war tradition and pacificism can be found. Cause for just war is summarized as follows for the Nephites:

> Nevertheless, the Nephites were inspired by a better cause; for they were not fighting for monarchy nor power. But they were fighting for their homes, and their liberties, their wives, and their children, and their all, and for their rites of worship and their church.
>
> And they were doing that which they felt was the duty which they owed to their God; for the Lord had said to them, and also to their fathers, "Inasmuch as ye are not guilty of the first offense, neither the second, ye shall not suffer yourselves to be slain by the hands of your enemies."
>
> And again, the Lord has said, "Ye shall defend your families, even to bloodshed"; therefore were the Nephites contending with the Lamanites, to defend themselves, and their families, and their lands, their country, and their rights, and their religion.—Alma 20:50-52

At another time and place, Mormon refuses to lead his people because they were motivated by the spirit of revenge (Mormon 1:80-81). Mormon's refusal illustrates another criteria for a just war—the absence of revenge.

Absolute pacifism is described in the story of those Lamanites converted by Nephite missionaries. These converted Lamanites buried their weapons of war and met unarmed the attacking soldiers of unconverted Lamanites. One thousand and five were slain with the spirit of praise on their lips, before their courageous witness so melted the hearts of the slaying soldiers that they were converted and laid down their arms (Alma 14:26-54). Ammon commented:

> For, behold, they had rather sacrifice their lives than even to take the life of their enemy, and they have buried their weapons of war deep in the earth because of their love toward their brethren.
>
> Now, behold, I say to you, Has there been so great love in all the land?
>
> Behold, I say to you, There has not, even among the Nephites.
>
> For, behold, they would take up arms against their brethren; they would not suffer themselves to be slain.
>
> But, behold, how many of these have laid down their lives; and we know that they have gone to their God because of their love, and of their hatred to sin.—Alma 14:118-122

After the appearance of the resurrected Christ the response of the Nephites was described as follows:

> And the thirty-fourth year passed away and also the thirty-fifth, and behold, the disciples of Jesus had formed a church of Christ in all the lands round about. And as many as came to them and truly repented of their sins were baptized in the name of Jesus; and they also received the Holy Ghost.
>
> And in the thirty-sixth year, the people were all converted to the Lord upon all the face of the land, both Nephites and Lamanites, and there were no contentions and disputations among them, and every man dealt justly one with another.
>
> And they had all things common among them, therefore they were not rich and poor, bond and free, but they were all made free and partakers of the heavenly gift. . . .
>
> And it came to pass that there was no contention in the land because of the love of God which dwelt in the hearts of the people. . . .

And surely there could not be a happier people among all the people who had been created by the hand of God.—IV Nephi 1-4, 17, 19

Although absolute pacifism does surface in the Book of Mormon and is commended, the just war tradition predominates.

In 1833, in the early days of the Restoration church, before word had been received of the hounding of the Saints out of Jackson County, Missouri, Joseph Smith gave this inspired counsel: "If ye will not abide in my covenant, ye are not worthy of me; therefore, renounce war and proclaim peace, and seek diligently to turn the hearts of the children to their fathers, and the hearts of the fathers to the children" (Doctrine and Covenants 95:3d). Joseph's counsel continues, however, to outline a form of the just war tradition which, nevertheless, commends complete restraint from violence (Doctrine and Covenants 95:5a-7g).

The early Saints, in response to continued persecution and harassment, became increasingly militant. First, there was the Zion's Camp expedition in 1834 to reclaim the Jackson County properties. This expeditionary force was stricken by fever and was also undermanned and ended on a peaceful note. Next, at Far West in 1838 Joseph Smith and Sidney Rigdon were in a much more militant mood, against both the enemies outside the church and dissenters within the church. It was at this time that the Danites—a secret terrorist force—began to operate within the church, a dark chapter in our history.

Later in 1838, war broke out between Mormons and "Gentiles." In the escalation of violence the church lost an apostle, David Patton; suffered a massacre, including small children and old men at

Haun's Mill; had an extermination order issued against them by Missouri Governor Lilburn Boggs, and, finally, saw the capture and imprisonment of many of the church leaders, including Joseph Smith and Sidney Rigdon. Only the courageous decision of General Alexander Doniphan to disobey his commanding officer saved them all from being shot. Then at Nauvoo, a new settlement of the regrouped church, the Latter Day Saints organized the Nauvoo Legion, a small private army with Joseph Smith as general in command. Again the blatant militancy of the Saints did little good in endearing them to their Gentile neighbors. Their aggressive postures clouded the moral case of the Saints and proved futile to save Joseph and Hyrum Smith from assassination in 1844 and the Saints' subsequent expulsion from Nauvoo.

The Reorganization, begun in 1852, was not militant, but Utah Mormonism continued to be so. Joseph Smith III, son of the assassinated prophet and later leader of the Reorganization, was faced with becoming a soldier in the American Civil War. He apparently decided it would be wrong to enlist as a volunteer but, if conscripted, felt he should go. He did not have to serve. It was under Joseph Smith III's kindly and tolerant leadership that the church adopted the following as its logo, the peace symbol inspired by Isaiah 11.

In the twentieth century, Reorganization president Frederick M. Smith supported and advocated church members doing military service when the United States entered hostilities in both world wars. Not all the Saints adopted his position. F. Henry Edwards—a British Saint who later became an apostle and a member of the First Presidency—became a conscientious objector in World War I. He served time in one of Britain's most notorious prisons for his witness, not knowing initially whether or not he would be shot. Later, after emigrating to America and with a closer relationship to Frederick M. Smith, he was not public about his views.

Thus, it would be true to say that the just war tradition has predominated in the Restoration movement and in the later Reorganization. Our movement then shares the just war tradition with the majority of other Christians, both Catholic and Protestant. However, the Book of Mormon contains in its pages the stark and awful testimony of the terrible destruction wrought by unrestrained human violence. War is in no way glorified. It is always a disaster—even if sometimes pictured as the "lesser of two evils." We should remember also that two civilizations described in Book of Mormon history were totally destroyed by war. There is no more important warning to be heard today when all human civilization is threatened by nuclear weapons.

We now turn to examine the ultimate in war—nuclear weapons and the strategy of mutually assured destruction (MAD)—and to do so by the criteria developed over the centuries in the just war tradition.

Just War and Nuclear Weapons

Sider and Taylor in chapter 4 of their book

Nuclear Holocaust and Christian Hope[18] consider seven criteria for a just war. These criteria are used in the following comparison to evaluate the morality of nuclear war according to the just war tradition.

JUST WAR	TOTAL NUCLEAR WAR
Criterion 1: Last resort. War, to be just, has to be the last resort, after all other attempts at reconciliation have been made.	If the USSR launches a massive first strike against Europe or North America, then this criterion of war as last resort would be fulfilled and justify war against the Soviet Union.
Criterion 2: Just cause. The cause for which one fights must be clearly just and the opponent must clearly be in the wrong.	The political and religious freedoms in Western democratic societies are treasured values and so it could be argued that the West would have a just cause.
Criterion 3: Right attitudes. Revenge cannot be the motive for war. The motive has to be the restoration of justice.	A massive retaliatory strike cannot meet this criterion. It is motivated by vengeance and could not achieve the restoration of justice because of the almost complete destruction resulting.
Criterion 4: Prior declaration of war. War has to be declared in order to give the opponent an opportunity to abandon unjust activity and thus encourage the prevention of war.	Missiles take only twenty-four minutes to travel between Moscow and Washington, D.C. A formal declaration of war is thus impossible, although repeated warnings of retaliation, if attacked first, might arguably substitute for a declaration of war. However, a first strike by the United States or European

JUST WAR	TOTAL NUCLEAR WAR
	nuclear powers is *clearly ruled out* as immoral under this criterion for a just war.
Criterion 5: Reasonable hope of success. If there is not objectivity and a reasonable hope of attaining the desired moral and political goals—then it is wrong to fight. "There must be a reasonable probability that the thing for which one is fighting will not be destroyed in the process."[19]	Nuclear war would most certainly destroy any hope of preserving what we would be fighting for. Historian H. Butterfield has reminded us that "with modern weapons we could easily put civilization back a thousand years, while the course of a single century can produce a colossal transition from despotic regimes to a system of liberty."[20]
Criterion 6: Non-combatant immunity. Civilians should not be the target of any direct military action. Although it is recognized that some may be injured or killed as an unintended side effect.	According to one source, a large nuclear attack even on military and economic targets would kill 70-160 million Americans and 100 million Soviet citizens. With population centers also targeted, 190 million Americans and 130 million Soviets would die—virtually all of them non-combatants.[21] This criterion of "non-combatant immunity" has led a broad spectrum of Christians to conclude that all-out nuclear war must be prohibited. As evangelical Christian John Stott has stated, "Every Christian, whatever he may think of the possibility of a 'just' use of

JUST WAR	TOTAL NUCLEAR WAR
	conventional weapons, must be a nuclear pacifist."[22] Ikle, commenting on the strategy of mutually assured destruction (MAD) has said, "Our method of preventing nuclear war rests on a form of warfare universally condemned since the Dark Ages—the mass killing of hostages."[22]
Criterion 7: Proportionality. There must be a reasonable chance that the good results obtained from the war outweigh the horrible evils unleashed.	If one or both societies are destroyed in a nuclear exchange, the terrible evil that has resulted clearly outweighs any good theoretically achieved. In fact the effects of nuclear war between the United States and the USSR would not be confined to these two nations. Radioactive fallout, nuclear winter, as well as the gross disruption of the world's economy, would mean that many millions of others would die.

"According to the 'just war' tradition, a particular war is justified if all the above criteria are met."[23] As it is, possibly five of the seven criteria *cannot* be fulfilled by the use of nuclear weapons. Even if an initial, limited nuclear exchange occurred—against exclusively military targets—it is difficult to see how escalation to further exchanges could be prevented. It is not surprising that Christian leaders, both Catholic and Protestant, are virtually unanimous in their condemnation of nuclear weapons.

Conclusion

The Christian peace traditions have been described—in outline—over two thousand years of Christianity. The question raised by those belonging to a pacifist tradition would be: "Has the world and its violence overcome the original teachings of Jesus and compromised the heart of the gospel—the cross?" Those belonging to the just war tradition might ask: "Are pacifists too 'heavenly-minded' to be any earthly good? Are they withdrawing from the world and the responsibility to protect the weak and establish justice? Is it not a Christian's task to be so involved, even if that means a certain amount of ambiguity and compromise in an imperfect world?"

Thus might the respective positions remain entrenched, but for two major developments in the twentieth century. The first is the development of nuclear weapons and the strategy of mutually assured destruction (MAD). It can be argued that *all* Christians must be nuclear pacifists. The second is the development of the strategy of nonviolent resistance—an active, involved pacifism. This was pioneered by M. K. Gandhi, first in South Africa and then in India, against the British. The success of this pacifism in achieving Indian independence is undisputed. Martin Luther King, with others, demonstrated its effectiveness in the United States during the civil rights movement. Economic and political justice can be achieved nonviolently.

In our age, when human life is threatened with annihilation, we face a crucial choice, perhaps *the* crucial choice in human history. Will we choose the way of violence culminating in nuclear holocaust or the way of nonviolent resistance to evil in whatever form it occurs? As Jim Wallis has asked, "Will the

Bomb, or the Cross, be the symbol of our age?"

We shall eventually return to the vistas of hope opened up by nonviolent resistance. In the next chapter, however, we shall consider soberly—and in some detail—the costs of war and preparations for war.

STUDY QUESTIONS

1. How do you respond to *(a)* the early Christian witness of pacifism, and *(b)* the development of the just war theory after the emperor Constantine became Christian?
2. Can one limit "loving your enemies" to the personal sphere and adopt a different code when societies, races, or cultures are at war?
3. The Restoration movement has traditionally emphasized the importance of returning to the spirit of the early Christian church. Does this mean we should embrace the pacifism of the early church as the Mennonites and Quakers have done?
4. How would you describe the strengths and weaknesses of *(a)* pacifism, and *(b)* the just war tradition?
5. It has been argued that the use of nuclear weapons is immoral, according to both pacifist and just war traditions. How do you respond to this argument?
6. What do you think of the successes achieved through nonviolence by Mahatma Gandhi and Martin Luther King?
7. Is the issue of war and peace one of trusting in God or trusting in our own strength? Some say that nuclear weapons are metal idols we worship today for our security? Do you agree?
8. Reflect on ways the meaning of the cross could affect your Christian discipleship. If appropriate, share one way in which the cross could change your way of acting in the coming week.

NOTES

1. John Ferguson, *The Politics of Love: The New Testament and Non-Violent Revolution* (Cambridge: James Clarke and Co., 1973), 102.
2. Ronald Sider, *Christ and Violence* (Tring, Herts: Lion Publishing, 1980), 24.
3. M. K. Gandhi, cited in Ferguson, 105.
4. Jim Wallis, cited in R. J. Sider and Richard K. Taylor, *Nuclear Holocaust and Christian Hope* (London: Hodder and Staughton, 1983), 138.
5. Martin Hengel, cited in Sider and Taylor, 119.
6. Ibid.
7. G. B. Caird, cited in Ferguson, 22.
8. Ferguson, 24.
9. Tertullian, "On Patience," cited in Ferguson, 25.
10. Jurgen Moltmann, cited in Sider and Taylor, 27.
11. Sider and Taylor, 29.
12. These quotations are from Ferguson, 57-60.
13. These quotations are from Ferguson, 64.
14. These quotations are from Ferguson, 65.
15. James Douglas, cited in Ferguson, 67.
16. Joseph J. Fahey, *Peace, War and the Christian Conscience* (New York: The Christophers, 1982), 3.
17. Ibid., 5.
18. Sider and Taylor, chapter 4.
19. Sider and Taylor, 70.
20. Ibid., 77.
21. Ibid., 74, 75.
22. Ibid., 75.
23. Ibid., 70.

The world actually finds itself at a crossroads. It can either continue to pursue the arms race or it can move toward a more sustainable international economic and political order. It cannot possibly do both.

—*Report to UN Second Special Session on Disarmament*[1]

Every gun that is made, every warship launched, every rocket fired, signifies a theft from those who hunger and are not fed, from those who are cold and not clothed.

—*General Dwight D. Eisenhower*[2]

These are portentous times. The lives of many are being sacrificed unnecessarily to the gods of war, greed, and avarice. The land is being desecrated by the thoughtless waste of vital resources. You must obey my commandments and be in the forefront of those who would mediate this needless destruction while there is yet day.

—*W. Wallace Smith, 1972*[3]

CHAPTER 4
THE COSTS OF WAR AND PREPARATIONS FOR WAR

Opportunity Costs

This chapter is not good news, nor will it be pleasant or easy reading. It is easier for us to close our minds, much as an ostrich hides its head in the sand. However, to face the reality of the present costs of war and preparations for war can lead to commitment to do something about it. Christian commitment to peace can be profoundly strengthened by understanding the personal, economic, and social costs of war. Today, faced with the ultimate cost in war—nuclear holocaust—it is urgent as never before to live out the prophetic vision: turning swords into plowshares and spears into pruning hooks.[4]

In this chapter we will consider what economists call "opportunity costs." If I have one hundred dollars and spend it on a bicycle, that one hundred dollars is gone. I cannot spend it on things like food, a house, or new clothes. The food, a house, or new clothes are the opportunity cost of spending one hundred dollars on a bicycle. In the same way spending one hundred dollars on a gun means that I have to forego the opportunity cost of other things that one hundred dollars could buy. When money is spent on weapons, it has an opportunity cost: it cannot be spent on other things such as medicine, education, or food.

Following are some opportunity costs of military:

- The price of one tank could provide classrooms for 30,000 students or improved storage facilities for 100,000 tons of rice.[5]

- The cost of one Trident submarine is equal to the cost of a year's schooling for sixteen million children in developing countries.[6]
- More money is now spent on military activities worldwide than on education, medicine, or any other field of social endeavor.[7]
- The World Health Organization (WHO) spent $83 million over ten years to wipe out smallpox in the world—an amount that would not buy even one modern strategic bomber. WHO's plan to eradicate malaria—a major killer in the Third World—has been slowed by lack of funds. The $450 million cost is *less than half* of what the world spends *daily* for military purposes.[8]
- The equivalent of an entire year's budget for the United Nations and all its specialized agencies is spent on arms around the world every two days.[9]
- Global military spending in 1981 was equivalent to $110 for every man, woman, and child on earth. By comparison only six cents per person was spent on international peace-keeping efforts.[10]
- Global military research spending is more than the *total* amount spent on research in energy, health, pollution control, and agriculture.[11]
- Fifty million people work full time in armament programs throughout the world, while scarcely more than one thousand "full timers" work on disarmament.[12]
- Worldwide military expenditures average $19,300 per soldier compared with a public education expenditure of $380 per school age child.[13]
- In 1980 the "money required to provide adequate food, water, education, health and housing for everyone [in need] in the world [was] estimated at $17 billion a year. It is a huge sum of money. . . about as much as the world spends on arms every two weeks."[14]
- Every two seconds a child somewhere on earth dies of preventable disease or malnutrition; every two seconds the United States spends about $20,000 on war and preparations for war.[15]

The Costs of Increased United States Military Spending

Since 1980 the United States government has been

committed to substantially increasing defense spending. What are the costs? Who is suffering?

There is the cost to the taxpayer. When all costs connected with military spending are added up, it amounts to approximately 55 percent of federal income taxes in 1984.[16]

In the period 1981-1985, United States defense spending increased by 39 percent. In the same period there was a decline in spending for social security and medicare (-6 percent), and low income programs (-16 percent). Thus the poor and vulnerable in the United States are suffering.[17]

The United States economy is the world's largest, amounting to 25 percent of the world's wealth produced each year. Its effect on the rest of the world's economy is considerable. Thus the huge budget deficit of the United States federal government—partly due to increased defense spending—has raised world interest rates sky high. This has made the debt costs of Third World countries a devastating burden. The debt crisis of the Third World is also made worse by the economic policies of the United States and other industrialized nations which helped initiate the world's worst recession since the 1930s. In Britain, for example, citizens pay unusually high mortgage rates, partly because of United States economic policy and defense spending. More seriously, many Britons are unemployed. However, the most vulnerable in the Third World—women and children—are stunted, diseased, and starved as a result. Thus the rest of the world also suffers the consequences from increased military spending in the United States and other superpower nations.

The Cost of Military Spending and Economic Strength: The British Example

One of the most startling economic declines relative to other nations has been that of Britain since World War II. Then it was one of the world's strongest economies; today it has been described as "Western Europe's industrial slum."[18] Why this decline relative to other national economies?

A look at military expenditure in relationship to growth in industrial productivity perhaps gives a clue.

MILITARY BURDEN AND NATIONAL PRODUCTIVITY 1960–1973[19]

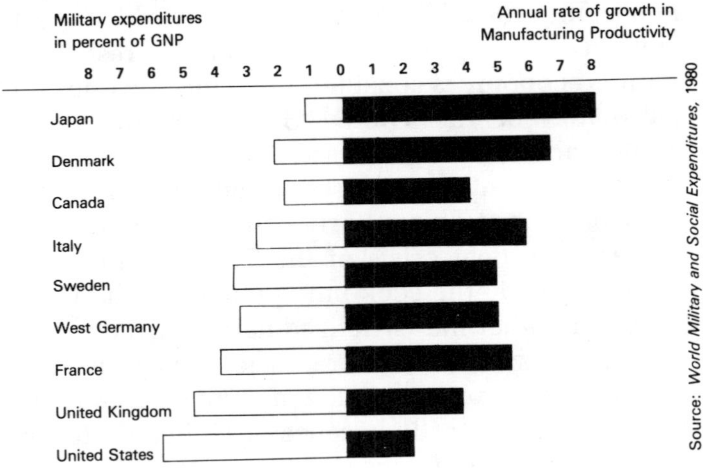

On one hand, Japan, which spends the least of any major industrialized country on defense because of its peace constitution, shows a remarkable rise in productivity. On the other hand, Britain and the United States—with the greatest defense costs—show the lowest increases in productivity. Both economies have been described as losers since the Second World War.

One researcher, Michael Chalmers, contends Britain's high military expenditure since World War II has indeed been responsible for Britain's industrial decline. Chalmers has identified a number of ways in which military spending has stunted economic growth, including these three:

1. Industrial investment has been sacrificed for military spending.
2. Technical progress in the civilian sector of the economy has been slowed by the disproportionate use of "scarce high-technology inputs, such as machine tools and scientific and engineering personnel" for military purposes.
3. The British balance-of-payments has suffered through expensive overseas military commitments and the diversion of resources from export industries. "This has in turn resulted in 'stop-go' policies of economic management which has reduced the incentives to invest and thus long term growth potential."[20]

As long ago as 1956 the highly respected magazine, the *Economist,* warned: "The heaviest cost of defense to the modern British economy . . . is not the 10 percent that it takes of the national income. It is the 60 percent that defense pre-empts of all the resources this country can assemble to invest in technological progress."[21]

The British government has continued to spend more than half its scientific budget on military research and development. In the 1980s the government continues to increase military spending, cut overseas aid, and allow more than 16 percent of the working population to be unemployed. Britain's sad decline is set to continue, sacrificed to continuing illusions of imperial grandeur.

Employment

Often the impetus for military spending is kept up by the appeal to jobs—that making armaments is good for employment. However, as has been pointed out in a United Nations report, "Today, there is rapidly accumulating evidence that high military budgets, instead of alleviating overall unemployment contribute substantially to it."[22]

The production of military equipment is more and more capital intensive, which means fewer and fewer jobs are created for the amount of money invested. It has become clear that given the same money civilian spending creates more jobs:

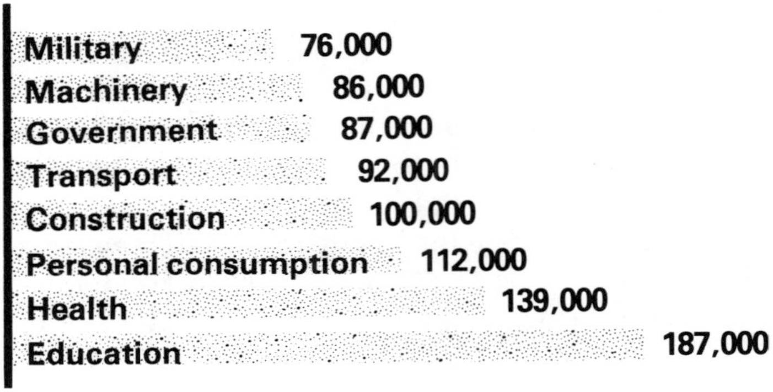

Total number of jobs generated by spending $1000 million in each area. (*Source: U.S. Bureau of Labor Statistics*)[23]

Thus, high military spending contributes to a nation's unemployment. In addition, employment within the armaments industry is fraught with insecurity, dependent upon contracts from the home government and overseas buyers which are susceptible to sudden cancellation. Finally, high military spending increases inflation; military goods are non-productive, they cannot produce wealth as investment in industry would.

This means, however, good news for those who advocate disarmament:

Disarmament has often been seen as an economic threat; in fact high military spending damages the economy and any effort to reverse the pattern of military spending presents an economic opportunity. . . . With careful planning, no one need suffer in the transition from military to civil work.[24]

The conversion of swords into plowshares and spears into pruning hooks would, in conclusion, not only *feed* more people but would also *employ* more people.

Military Costs in the Third World

One of the present tragedies is that Third World countries spend almost twice as much on their armed forces as they do on health and education combined.[25] Some national examples will make this tragic point even clearer:

INDIA. Expenditure per soldier was $3,192* as against $5 on education and $2 on health for a population of over 650 million, the fourth largest in the world. India has 1,096,000 in the armed forces against 178,000 physicians and 3 million teachers. Literacy rate is 36 per cent, infant mortality rate 134,000, and 70 per cent of the population does not have safe water.

TANZANIA. Public expenditure per soldier was $6,370 against $12 on education and $5 on health. There are 27,000 soldiers against 800 physicians, and 4,700 teachers for a population of 17 million. Literacy rate is 60 per cent and infant mortality rate 125 for every 1000 births. Nearly 60 per cent of the population does not have safe water.

ARGENTINA. Public expenditure per soldier was $11,000 against $54 on education and $11 on health. There are 133,000

*Note: dollar amounts in U.S. currency

soldiers compared to 51,000 physicians and 259,000 teachers for a population of 27 million. Literacy rate is 94 per cent, infant mortality rate 45 for every 1000 births, and 34 per cent of the population does not have access to safe water.[26]

In terms of Third World economics it has been calculated that every dollar spent on defense *reduces* agricultural output by twenty cents. The tragedy of such wasteful spending has been escalating. Between 1969 and 1978 arms sales increased twenty times to Africa and by three times to Latin America. Third World countries now import 75 percent of all armament exports.[27]

What are the causes of such high military spending in the Third World?[28]

First there is the legacy of colonization. Decolonization left boundary disputes that have caused tensions, conflicts, and local arms races. Examples are India and Pakistan, Israel and neighboring Arab nations, North and South Vietnam, Turkey and Greece, Taiwan and China, China and India, and South Africa and neighboring states. In addition, when colonized, the country was disarmed, so when independence came, re-armament was thought to be justified.

Then there is superpower rivalry. After the Second World War, countries within zones of influence established by the superpowers were encouraged to arm, often initially provided free by the superpower concerned. Thus, superpower rivalry between the Soviet Union and the United States has been responsible for increasing armament expenditure in the Third World. The following graphs show the shares of the two superpowers in armament exports:

The Soviet and U.S. shares of world exports of major weapons: total exports and exports to the Third World, 1979-83[29]

Today both superpowers are about equally contributing to 60 percent of the military exports to the Third World. Other major exporters include France, Britain, West Germany, and Italy.

The third cause of high military spending is that Western development experts in the 1950s and 1960s saw modernization of the armed forces as a powerful key to development.

The arms exporters permit conflicts to continue. For instance the current Iran-Iraq war in the Middle East would have been halted had it been possible to organize an effective arms embargo to both countries. This helps reinforce the point that high levels of military expenditure in the Third World—whether in war or in peace—are partly the responsibility of the United States, Soviet, and European suppliers.

What Frederick M. Smith pointed out in the 1930s is still true today: "The arms manufacturers are our real international villains and traitors."[30]

There is a further, sinister twist to the high military spending in the Third World. Often the armed forces are not mobilized against an external enemy but in repression of the nation's own people and democratic aspirations.

There are some 126 countries in the Third World. At the last count, 56 were under *direct* military rule. There were two coups on 24 March 1982, Bangladesh and Guatemala. Approximately three-quarters of the men who received their military training in the USA and the USSR belong to those countries which have witnessed 81 coups since 1960. Possibly a coincidence, probably a cause.[31]

A spiral of increasing repression and poverty can be set in motion which is difficult to change.

The Poverty-Repression-Militarization Cycle[32]

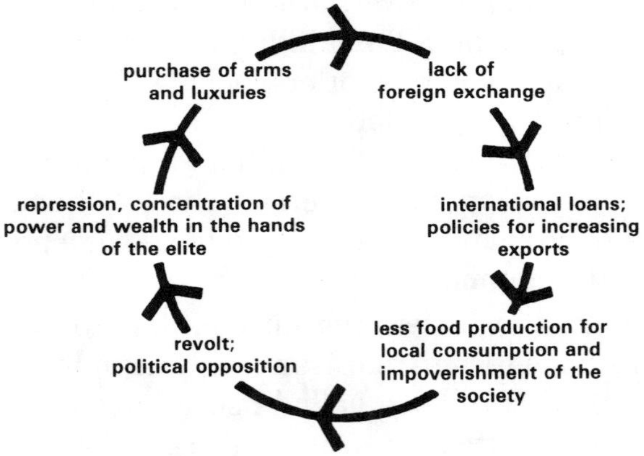

This further increases the suffering of the poor and vulnerable in the Third World. It is reported that Britain, the mother of parliamentary democracy, is the world's second largest exporter of military equipment. In recent years Britain has sold arms to more than forty countries listed by Amnesty International as having violated human rights.[33] This pattern is unfortunately repeated by other Western democracies, including the United States.

Economic Aid and Military Spending

The amount of economic aid given compared with world military expenditure is shown in the following graph.[34]

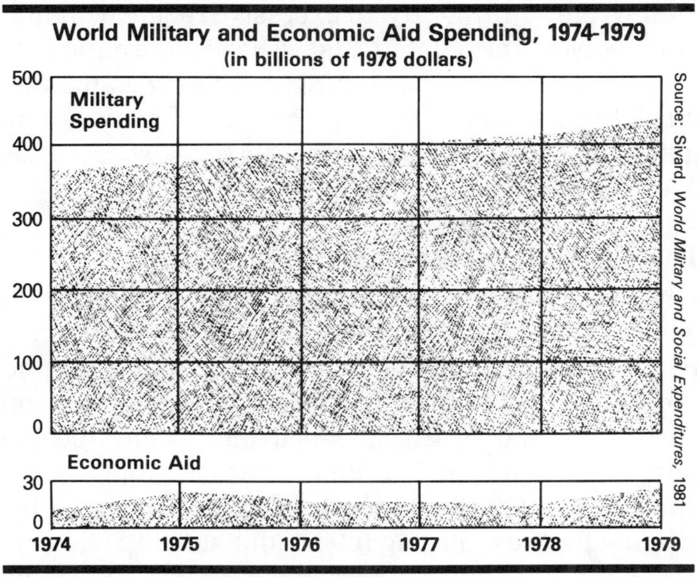

Economic aid is only a fraction of world military expenditure. This tragedy is reinforced by the fact that so little additional economic aid is needed to make a significant difference. "One-half of one percent (0.5 percent) of one year's world military expenditures would pay for all the farm equipment needed to increase food production and approach self-sufficiency in food-deficit, low-income countries by 1990."[35]

Unfortunately, in the 1980s United States overseas aid has shown almost a doubling of security (military) aid at the expense of stagnating levels of development assistance.[36] United States aid is given according to United States strategic interests rather than according to need or justice. This is no more clearly shown than in United States aid to Pakistan.[37]

It is with some degree of accuracy that Arthur Simon wrote in 1974, "By an excessive reliance on military power, the United States has undermined its capacity to reduce world hunger. As long as the politics of power rather than the politics of justice dominates our thinking, we will do little to assist countries overwhelmed by poverty."[38]

The Costs of Nuclear War

Nuclear weapons account for about 20 percent of global military expenditure. If used, however, they result in the ultimate cost. It is sufficient to remind each one of us that each bomb dropped in 1945 on Hiroshima and Nagasaki killed more than 100,000 people outright and inflicted severe injuries on another 125,000. Today the total explosive power belonging to an expanding international club of owners is equal to one million Hiroshima bombs, the equivalent of three tons of conventional explosive for every person on earth.[39]

It is estimated that between 5,000 and 10,000 megatons would be exploded in a nuclear war. The results have been described as follows:

[More than] 1 billion people would be killed outright in such a nuclear war, mainly in the United States, the Soviet Union, Europe, China and Japan. An additional 1.1 billion people would suffer serious injuries and radiation sickness, for which medical help would be unavailable. It thus seems possible that more than 2 billion people—almost half of all the humans on earth—would be destroyed in the immediate aftermath of a global thermonuclear war. This would represent by far the greatest disaster in the history of the human species.[40]

Unfortunately this probably underestimates the consequences of nuclear war. It appears that clouds of dust and smoke released into the atmosphere following a nuclear war would, in the Northern Hemisphere, block out the sun sufficiently to cause a nuclear winter. Land temperatures would drop to -25°C (13°F) for months on end, even if war occurred in the summer, killing most crops and animals. Most survivors would starve if they did not die of epidemics or cold first. Finally, scientists believe nuclear winter could be initiated by 100 megatons of nuclear bombs—a mere one-sixth of the world's stock.[41]

Vast clouds of dust would drift across the equator to also darken and cool the Southern Hemisphere. The almost complete disruption of the integrated world economy would result in widespread famines—even in uninvolved nations south of the equator. Those surviving famine may yet perish in political instabilities and local wars.

Thus, the accumulations of thousands of years of human civilization and countless aeons of biological evolution would be destroyed in one sickening, searing, awful day. Derelict, cratered cities and radioactive hills, valleys, and plains could no longer echo with the joyous chatter of little children. They would be no more. Generations that could have been would not be. Evil would have triumphed because parents and grandparents, aunts and uncles, did too little or nothing at all.

Conclusion

The human costs of war and preparations for war are enormous. Nuclear war would be the ultimate cost. The pain, suffering, and terror in individual stories are not calculable. Even now, without bullets being fired or missiles launched, people are being killed because of the tragic diversion of scarce resources from agriculture, education, and medicine—all to military purposes.

Having been renewed in awareness about the seriousness of present human history we now turn to look more earnestly at the ways that foster peace and equality.

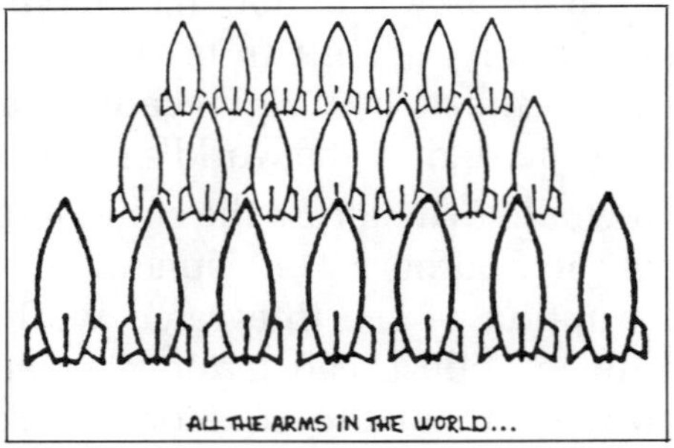

—Used by permission of *New Internationalist,* 42 Hythe Bridge Street, Oxford OXI 2EP, United Kingdom

STUDY QUESTIONS

1. What, if any, have been the personal costs of war in your family's history?
2. Does understanding the costs of war and preparations for war paralyze you or does it strengthen your Christian commitment to peace?
3. How do you react to the possibility of nuclear war?
4. In what ways can our many emotions about war—especially nuclear war—be usefully channelled?
5. Most governments around the world probably spend more on war and preparations for war than Saints would like. In what ways can you begin changing that in your nation? What organizations do you know which could help you?
6. Should Saints, like early Christians, think seriously about working for the military or in armaments production? Are there any special stewardship and witnessing opportunities for Saints working in these forms of employment or is their discipleship inevitably compromised?
7. Why do you think so much is spent on armaments?
8. Does the following take on new meaning and a more urgent call for you after reading this chapter?

> These are portentous times. The lives of many are being sacrificed unnecessarily to the gods of war, greed, and avarice. The land is being desecrated by the thoughtless waste of vital resources. You must obey my commandments and be in the forefront of those who would mediate this needless destruction while there is yet day.
>
> —Doctrine and Covenants 150:7

NOTES

1. Cited in "Disarmament-Development," *Links Magazine* (September 1983): 32.
2. Cited in "Disarmament-Development," 2.
3. Doctrine and Covenants 150:7.
4. See Isaiah 2:4 and Micah 4:3.
5. Cited in Oxfam America, "Facts for Action" in *Outreach on Hunger Resource Materials* (Washington, D.C.: Bread for the World Educational Fund, 1985), 18.
6. P.D. Bishop, *A Technique for Loving: Non-violence in Indian and Christian Traditions* (London: SCM Press, 1984), 152.
7. *The Arms Race or the Human Race? A Choice for Mankind* (New York: United Nations Department of Public Information, 1981), 2.
8. *The Arms Race or the Human Race?* 10.
9. Bishop, 152.
10. *New Internationalist Magazine* (March 1983): 10.
11. Ibid., 11.
12. Ted Lentz, "Communication to the Editor," *The Journal of Conflict Resolution* XVI, no. 4 (December 1972): 622, 623.
13. *New Internationalist Magazine* (March 1983): 10.
14. *New Internationalist Magazine* (January 1980).
15. Elaboration of statement made by Sheldon Stahl, Lecture on "Militarism and Hunger," *Bread for the World Educational Fund Seminar,* RLDS Central Congregation, Kansas City, Saturday, April 19, 1985.
16. This computation is based on figures submitted to the United States Congress by the president on February 1, 1985. Calculations done by Friends Committee on National Legislation in Washington, D.C., based on the "federal funds" budget.
17. "Where the Budget Has Grown" in *Outreach on Hunger Resource Materials,* 66.
18. Malcolm Chalmers, *The Cost of Britain's Defence* (University of Bradford: Peace Studies Papers, no. 10, May 1983), 5.
19. *New Internationalist Magazine* (March 1981): 25.
20. Chalmers, 5.
21. Ibid., 30.
22. *The Arms Race or Human Race?* 12.

23. Leaflet, "Choices," produced by CAAT, 11, Goodwin Street, London, N4 3HQ. See also *Priorities: A Bimonthly Discussion of Alternatives to a Military Economy,* June 1976 issue on Jobs and Military Spending (American Friends Service Committee, 980 North Fair Oaks Avenue, Pasadena, California 91103).
24. Alternative Defence Commission, *Threat or Opportunity: the Economic Consequences of Non-nuclear Defence* (Bradford University: Peace Research Reports, no. 6, September 1984), 61.
25. "How Much Does a Soldier Cost?" *South: The Third World Magazine* (July 1982): 8.
26. Ibid., 8, 9.
27. *Outreach on Hunger Resource Materials,* 138.
28. For the following conclusions to this question I am indebted to an article "The Myth of the 'Man on Horseback,'" *South: The Third World Magazine* (July 1982): 10, 11.
29. *Armaments or Disarmament? Sipri Summary, 1984* (Stockholm International Peace Research Institute), 28.
30. F. M. Smith, "Nationalism and War," *Saints' Herald* 84, no. 48 (November 27, 1937): 1507.
31. "The Myth of the 'Man on Horseback,'" 11.
32. Committee on Poverty and the Arms Trade, *Bombs for Breakfast,* Second Edition, 1981, 20.
33. Leaflet, "The Repression Trade," CAAT, 11 Goodwin Street, London, N4 3HQ.
34. *Outreach on Hunger Resource Materials,* 144.
35. Ibid., 19.
36. Ibid., 139.
37. Bread for the World, *Notes from O/L Discussion Case Study: Pakistan.*
38. Cited in *Outreach on Hunger Resource Materials,* 143.
39. *Arms Race or Human Race?* 4.
40. Cited by Carl Sagan, "The Nuclear Winter," *Parade Magazine* (October 30, 1983): 4.
41. Ibid., 4, 5, 7.

Whether or not Christianity, in an alienated, divided and oppressive society, itself becomes alienated, divided and an accomplice of oppression, is ultimately decided only by whether the crucified Christ is a stranger to it or the Lord who determines the form of its existence.[1]

—Jurgen Moltmann

There is neither Jew nor Greek, there is neither slave nor free, there is neither male nor female; for you are all one in Christ Jesus.

—Paul the Apostle (Galatians 3:28 RSV)

If there be righteousness in the heart,
there will be beauty in the character.
If there is beauty in the character,
there will be harmony in the home.
If there is harmony in the home,
there will be order in the nation.
When there is order in each nation,
there will be peace in the world.

—Old Chinese Proverb

CHAPTER 5
EMPOWERING VISTAS

The Cross: God Is Committed

Remember the worth of souls is great in the sight of God; for behold, the Lord your Redeemer suffered death in the flesh; wherefore he suffered the pain of all men, that all men might repent and come unto him.—Doctrine and Covenants 16:3c

The Cross is an anchor to our values: people are precious—too precious to be destroyed on the battlefield or by neglect or injustice. In the Cross the evil of humanity is vividly displayed. There is no idealization of noble humanity, for we are seen in all our awfulness. Yet it is here we find opportunity to change because we are confronted by a love, wisdom, and innocence that disturbs profoundly.

Yet as we are reminded in John 3:16, Christ died not only for humanity but for the whole world, for all of life on our green and blue planet that hurtles silently through space. How dare we continue to rape and pollute the fragile web of life that enfolds our earthly home. How dare we threaten countless species—including our own—with extinction, when it has taken millions of patient years to create them in all their wondrous glory.

The Cross, however, confronts us not with oughts and moral indignation—although this is part of its power. Above all, the Cross confronts us with grace—the security of unconditional love—which accepts us as we are and yet empowers us to be converted when Easter hope begins to rise in us. "Love releases the power to love."[2]

Christians are those who have sensed that they are unconditionally loved and are also committed to be gracious. The cross of Christ, when accepted, brings the Sermon on the Mount to life in us. "Love your enemies" breaks the spiral of violence in crosses which creates new peaceful possibilities in individual and collective histories.

The Cross is foolishness to the powerful and a stumbling block to the oppressor, but it is the power and wisdom of God.[3] The Cross is "the test of everything which deserves to be called Christian."[4] The Cross is above all the test of faithfulness. If Christian people in a hungry, violent world are affluent and support by votes, skills, or apathy an unjust economy or their nation's war machine, it is because the crucified God is no longer Lord, but a stranger to them.

The Cross is God's peace initiative to the world. No other kind of initiative—divine or human—can save us. The Sermon on the Mount, the spirit and ethic of the Cross, too long has been considered utopian by Christians. The ineffectiveness of mainstream Western Christianity, both Catholic and Protestant, is shown by the fact that it was a Hindu in India by the name of Gandhi who demonstrated persuasively that the spirit and ethic of the Cross worked. His victory over an oppressive British rule was won by integrity, truth, kindness, and peaceful resistance. His victory was a double one, for he won many British to his side also.

The crucified God is committed to our salvation, to redeeming a hungry, violent, and endangered world. We need not ask God to support us in our efforts for it is God who has already gone before us and calls us to follow. To follow is to have opened the vista of the empowering cross.

Universal Vision

Human diversity of culture, race, and giftedness is an opportunity for enrichment in the same way as the diversity of flowers in a garden blesses us with contrasting colors, scents, and foliage. Yet in a fallen world human diversity often divides and alienates us from one another.

It has been my privilege to work among and visit nations and peoples in Europe, Asia, and the Americas. In all our wonderful diversity, which is not always comfortable, there is a common humanness in us—no matter our history. We laugh at what is funny; we cry with the same hurts; we are uplifted by beauty and excellence. The tragedies of hunger and sickness and the joys of marriage and birth feel the same in all of us.

One of the special gifts of Jesus' ministry was uncovering this common humanity in different and fallen people. In the Roman centurion, the fallen woman, the leper, the cursing fisherman, the Jewish freedom fighter, and the arrogant Pharisee, Jesus uncovered a human being—frightened and insecure, as well as gifted with the potential for love and wholeness. Jesus persisted in showing us that even our "fallenness" unites us when we recognize it in ourselves as well as in our neighbor. In having their common humanness revealed by Jesus, some responded with tears of uncontrollable joy. Others, with a sense of hardened superiority, sometimes were bitterly outraged.

Jesus' sense of *universalism*—the equal, wonderful worth of every human—was not new. He only made more personal what was already understood in the magnificent writings of Isaiah (chapters 40-55) which contain the glorious affirmations of the One

Living God, Creator and Savior of all the world.

I am the Lord, and there is no other, besides me there is no God; I gird you, though you do not know me, that men may know, from the rising of the sun and from the west, that there is none besides me; I am the Lord, and there is no other. . . . And there is no other god besides me, a righteous God and a Savior; there is none besides me. Turn to me and be saved, all the ends of the earth! For I am God, and there is no other.—Isaiah 45:5-6, 21-22 RSV

With an affirmation of the One God of all the earth dawns the realization by Isaiah that Yahweh is God not only of Israel but of all people. The people of Israel are saved and chosen not merely for their own sake, but for the sake of the Gentiles, to be a servant and instrument of Yahweh's salvation. Thus Yahweh says to Israel: "I will give you as a light to the nations that my salvation may reach to the end of the earth" (Isaiah 49:6 RSV). We are thus profoundly indebted to Jewish prophetic insight, made flesh in Jesus, for a vista of the whole human family as one.

The opposite of universalism is *parochialism*. Instead of seeing that all are a part, yet together comprising a greater and more wonderful whole, we assert that our own family, nation, or history is the best or only way to see things. My parochial views in growing up included a belief that the British are better than anybody else (though the northern English were better than the southern English). As regarding human standards our family preserved the best. Such attitudes are harmless enough on the playing field, but suicidal in a nuclear conflict.

The ultimate sin in the parochial attitude is self-centeredness. Its opposite is universalism—sacrificial love for one's neighbor, whoever is found in need. Our family, religious, or national parochialisms are simply examples of collective self-centeredness. This parochialism—individually and collectively—was eclipsed with God's self-giving love in Christ. It clashed with the Cross. Universal love exposed and defeated the darkness and selfish evil of parochialism by showing that God's love is greater than our selfishness.

The developing reality of a worldwide fellowship of Restoration Christians is a faithful response to the universal Christ. Some of my own most enriching and challenging experiences have come in international gatherings that have been facilitated by our growing church. The World Church is an international fellowship working for a global vision that calls us from our sins of parochialism and self-centeredness, to be accountable to each other for peace and justice. The greater desire for interfaith sharing among our people and the move to more fully recognize the gifts of women are responses to the universal Christ also. Yet we are called to extend our response to the universal Christ by more seriously reflecting on our attitudes and our affluence in a violent, hungry world.

The widening vista of universalism is seen from the Cross—all humans are part of one family. All humans are of unique worth, created and redeemed to be equal in dignity and resources for an abundant life. And because it is reported that nature itself was darkened and shook at the Crucifixion, the Cross points also to the fact that humanity is part of one ecology of life, set in one universe of creation and redemption.

Spirit, Equality, and Peace

The writers of the American Declaration of Independence asserted, "We hold these truths to be self-evident, that all men are created equal." If that created equality is lost in a fallen world, it is the Christian testimony that all persons are redeemed equally. Equality follows from the redeemed worth of persons and is the parallel of universalism. Equality is the vigorous assertion made repeatedly by the Judeo-Christian tradition. It is the heart of the testimony of the Restoration.

As Isaiah writes, the outworkings of the Spirit of the Lord in the Messiah result in equality and righteousness; the fruits of equality and righteousness are peace.

> And the Spirit of the Lord shall rest upon him. . . . With righteousness he shall judge the poor, and decide with equity for the meek of the earth. . . . The wolf shall dwell with the lamb, and the leopard shall lie down with the kid, and the calf and the lion and the fatling together and a little child shall lead them.—Isaiah 11:2, 4, 6 RSV

> The Spirit is poured upon us from on high. . . . Then justice will dwell in the wilderness, and righteousness abide in the fruitful field. And the effect of righteousness will be peace, and the result of righteousness, quietness and trust forever.—Isaiah 32:15-17 RSV

It is also appropriate to remember that the Hebrew word *shalom* represents both well-being and peace. This same holistic view of Messiah, Spirit, righteousness, and peace is described in the Book of Mormon.

> And the thirty-fourth year passed away and also the thirty-fifth, and, behold, the disciples of Jesus had formed a church of Christ in all the lands round about. And as many as came to them and truly repented of their sins were baptized in the name of Jesus; and they also received the Holy Ghost. And in the thirty-sixth year, the people were all converted to the Lord upon all the face of the land, both Nephites and Lamanites, and there were no contentions and disputations among them, and every man dealt justly one with another. And they had all things in common among them, therefore they were not rich and poor, bond and

free, but they were all made free and partakers of the heavenly gift. . . . And it came to pass that there was no contention in the land because of the love of God which dwelt in the hearts of the people. . . . And surely there could not be a happier people among all the people who had been created by the hand of God.—IV Nephi 1:2-4, 17, 19

In another culture and wisdom, the Chinese character

平

has two meanings: peace and levelling or equality. Thus peace is correlated with equality in that culture. This same symbol is used on our church seal throughout Asia where Chinese characters are understood.

The ancients may correlate equality and peace, but what do modern social scientists and scholars find? Paul Harrison, an authority on the Third World, has noted:

Resource shortages and internal social conflicts have been causes of most of the wars in history. Once again we should note that the world's pacifist nations—Sweden, Switzerland, Costa Rica—all enjoy social peace at home based on participatory democracies inherited from egalitarian, small holding peasants.[5]

Harrison is not alone. The peace scientist Francis A. Beer states:

There are powerful arguments relating war and inequality. Violence has been associated with injustice, and injustice with inequality, in Western political theory since its beginnings. Many modern social scientists of conflict—Marx, Freud, Simmel, Pareto, Michels, Mannheim, Lasswell, Mills, Coser, Dahrendorf, Marcuse, Edelman, Galtung—have shown in detail the way that structures and processes of domination and subordination imply direct or indirect violence. It seems obvious that violence leads to inequality. There are no historical records, says Andreski, "of military victories where the conquerors acquired no privileges" (1968:40). Existing inequalities, on the other hand, provide a very powerful incentive for violence.[6]

David Thompson states that "world politics are now, to a great extent the result of a clash between conditions of inequality and ideals of equality."[7]

Equality and genuine peace are inseparably connected in scriptural insight, Asian wisdom, and scholarly observation. The issues of poverty and violence are not two separate unrelated issues; they are two sides of the same coin. Without one you do not have the genuine other. Whether we focus on making the world more equal or work for resolving conflicts nonviolently and on the side of justice, we are engaged in the single cause of building community, the cause of Zion, where peace shall yet be.

In contrast to the spiral of war which results from injustice aggravating violent conflict, and violent conflict making for greater injustice (illustrated below)

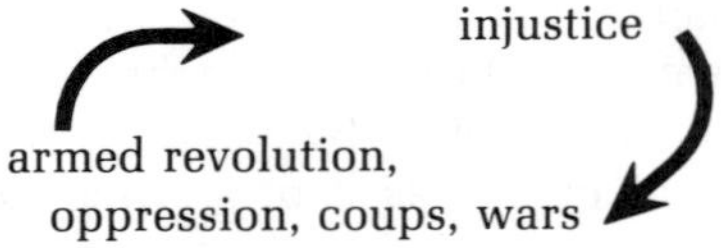

Spiral of Violence

we move into the spiral of peace.

Spiral of Peace

The vista of Zion, global peace initiated by communities of committed disciples, uplifts our hopes with the promise of giftedness and power to accompany us in that task: "Blessed are they who shall seek to bring forth my Zion at that day, for they shall have the gift and the power of the Holy Ghost. And whoso shall publish peace, even tidings of great joy, how beautiful upon the mountains shall they be" (I Nephi 3:187, 189).

Little Children Can Lead Us

For two years my family lived in Japan, where my wife, Jewell, and I taught in the church's school in Tokyo. I discovered, as a tall, hairy Anglo-Saxon, that I was somewhat threatening to Japanese people. For my part I had some fears about Japanese men, arising from the horror stories I had heard from the Second World War. What would help us meet and begin to trust each other?

The go-between was our year-old son, Matthew. With Matthew in my arms or with me on my bicycle, I was no longer so intimidating. For my part the responsive twinkle in the eyes of some Japanese men to Matthew communicated that they, too, knew what it meant to be a father. So it was through Matthew as a toddler that we got to know all the neighbors on our street. And through the children we taught in the school we were able to meet and be trusted by many more people in the community.

We are disarmed by little children, no matter their race or nationality. It is their innocence, their undisputed worth, and their right to grow up whole and unafraid that can yet motivate us to do something better.

Indeed the welfare of little children can provide

us with a guide to right and wrong that lifts us high above the swirling deceptions of ideology and nationalism. If what I do threatens, harms, or makes little children afraid, then it is *wrong* beyond any shadow of doubt. If what I do contributes to a world where little boys and girls can grow up whole and unafraid then it is *right*. We are indeed making a better world when it becomes safer for children everywhere.

It is no small wonder that Jesus focused the meaning of the kingdom and personal fulfillment upon little children. He reflected in his ministry to both Jews and Nephites that picture of peace described by Isaiah: "The wolf shall dwell with the lamb, and the leopard shall lie down with the kid, and the calf and the lion and the fatling together, and a little child shall lead them" (Isaiah 11:6 RSV).

The Personal God

I remember the words of a song—"God is real, God is real, God is real to me"—that came into my mind the first time I recognized the presence of the Holy Spirit in my life. As a person exploring the church, first in Germany and later Wales, I had been impressed by ordinary people who humbly testified of the reality of God in their life experience. I believed their stories because I was persuaded by their integrity, honesty, and the extra "something" I sensed in their lives. But could God be real to *me*? Perhaps, if I but believed. I wept tears of surprised joy when one evening, while driving my old red Volkswagen I suddenly sensed God's presence in my relationships with other church people, and—at the same time—in me.

Restoration Christians in every generation, together with many others, have testified in personal ways of a living Christ who is transforming lives and creating community. Today many things may lead us to doubt or neglect these precious experiences with the Spirit of Christ. However, the awesome task of building a world community safe for little children everywhere means that we allow and give time for Christ to deepen that reality in us and between us.

The Cause of Zion

Zion, the kingdom of God on earth, is the melody of the Restoration movement. Without the vision and commitment of our people to Zion our history is scarcely worth telling.[8] It indeed has been our testimony that heaven is touching earth for those with faith to see and that a marvelous work and wonder is indeed about to break forth.

True, our vision of Zion has at times been parochial, ethnocentric, and even nationalistic. But there has always been a universalistic heart to our kingdom dream. Every time we say the Lord's Prayer we are reminded that Zion is to be global: "Thy kingdom come, thy will be done, on earth as it is in heaven" (Matthew 6:10 RSV).

It is for each new generation to renew the vision of the kingdom handed on to them. The vision needs to be renewed today in our own experience of the Spirit of Christ amidst the turbulence and opportunities of history in our own time. If we see further and wider than those who have gone before, it is because we stand on their shoulders. It is also because God has yet more light and truth to break forth in our day.

There are no idols in the coming Zion, nothing that betrays the ultimate worth of persons. Nothing made by human hands or created in human minds is worshiped here; all things can be undone that cripple or deform the human personality. There is a continual renewal and rebuilding of all human structures—social, economic, and political—to enable the potential for goodness, beauty, and truth to grow and flower in all. Zion is beginning whenever people individually and collectively are achieving their God-given potential to love, be creative, and live joyously. Zion is beginning right where we are when an enlarging global vision causes us to invest ourselves in creating righteousness in our local communities.

In this task we are not alone. The promise is given in that remarkable beatitude in the Book of Mormon: "Blessed are they who shall seek to bring forth my Zion at that day, for they shall have the gift and power of the Holy Ghost" (I Nephi 3:187).

This promise has renewed my hope and strength many times as I am reminded that the task of creating a world safe for little children everywhere is not ours alone. We are joined by the Spirit of the Christ who became a child two millenia ago.

Zion the beautiful beckons us on. It is a dream and potential reality that is worth giving our all to and for. It is significant that recent direction to the church counsels us: "The call is for workers in the cause of Zion; therefore neither tarry nor doubt that I am" (Doctrine and Covenants 155:8).

STUDY QUESTIONS

1. What meaning does the Cross have for you?
2. What hymns do you know that speak of a global vision or universal Christ? If appropriate, share a place and time when a hymn with a universal message had special meaning for you. (You may wish to sing one or more verses of a hymn together.)
3. What scriptures would you describe as pointing to universalism? Can you think of examples of parochialism?
4. Give examples of attitudes that you used to have which you now think are parochial.
5. How do you react to the World Church being defined as an international fellowship working for a global vision? Give some examples of parochialism with which the church is now struggling.
6. If we are called first to be citizens of the kingdom how does this affect our national citizenship and other local loyalties?
7. Do you agree with the assertion that spirit, equality, and peace are inseparably connected? What challenges or questions could you or others raise against this assertion? What truth is there for the assertion in your opinion?
8. What are the opportunities and pitfalls of the concept of a global Zion initiated by networks of communities of people, all over the planet, dedicated to creating a more just and peaceful world?
9. In what ways has Christ been real to you? How have you been changed as a result?
10. In what ways does Christ uplift and strengthen you personally in discipleship?

NOTES

1. Jurgen Moltmann, *The Crucified God,* trans. R. A. Wilson and J. Bowden (SCM Press: London, 1976), 3.
2. Aleah G. Koury, Sermon, Birmingham, United Kingdom, October 1973.
3. To paraphrase I Corinthians 1:23-25.
4. Moltmann, 7.
5. Paul Harrison, *The Third World Tomorrow* (Middlesex: Pelican, 1980), 350.
6. Francis A. Beer, *Peace Against War* (San Francisco: W. H. Freeman and Company, 1981), 170.
7. David Thompson, ed., *Political Ideas* (Middlesex: Penguin Books, reprinted 1980), 200, 201.
8. Inez Smith Davis, *The Story of the Church* (Independence, Missouri: Herald House, sixth edition, 1959), 12.

We preach a vision, and work for every inch.

—Paul Nelson, Bread for the World[1]

Human salvation lies in the hands of the creatively maladjusted.

—Martin Luther King[2]

Everywhere there are visionaries and a visionary is fine—if he sees the bridge to his vision.

—Brock Chisholm, former director-general WHO[3]

It is of little use to call for a very big change in values without at least incorporating these values in some new structures, no matter how small. Because as we know . . . in the beginning was the word, but then the word came and became flesh and dwelt among us.

—E. F. Schumacher[4]

One man awake
Can waken another
The second can waken
His next door brother
The three awake
Can rouse a town
By turning the whole
Place upside down
The many awake
Can make such a fuss
That it finally wakens
The rest of us!

One man up
With dawn in his eyes
Multiplies!

—*Anonymous*

CHAPTER 6
ENABLING ACTION

Now is the time to consider action and the quality of action which testifies in deed of the living Christ. There is no good news unless it is the good news of deed. As word became flesh in Christ so thought and conviction must be worked out and demonstrated in us. Faithfulness is not merely personal belief but social involvement in ways that are extensions of the crucified God's unconditional kindness.

Accountability to the Poor and Each Other

A major key to enabling effective action is holding ourselves accountable in measurable ways in the use of our resources, time, and energies. Accountability involves allowing others whom we trust to help us in judgment of ourselves. That may sound negative, but it is not. We must let others help us live up to our best desires, our inspired commitments. Discipleship is a social endeavor. As a log separated from the fire quickly goes out, so does a warm commitment quickly cool when alone and unsupported by others.

There are immense cultural pressures within us and around us that call for the maintenance of things as they are. It is easy to fall back into the conforming ways of an apathetic society if we are not supported by the fellowship of others also committed to working for peace and justice.

The support we need to share with each other is not legalistic. A "support group" or "network" is a gathering where the power to love unconditionally grows. It is here that we can be honest about our failures, knowing we shall not be condemned but shall be restored to discipleship once more, wiser from experience and grateful for the loving support which enables a new start. Thus we help each other sustain our commitment.

Accountability to a group alone is not sufficient. It is so easy for a group to become enclosed and develop its own special kind of parochialism. The group needs to be accountable to a wider and, if possible, international fellowship in order to share a vision which is more closely universal. That is why conferences—regional, national, and international—are so important. The international fellowship of the church, as well as other international movements, has, therefore, an important accountability function in our endeavors.

Yet this is still not sufficient. There must be concrete anchors providing guiding principles for our widening circles of human support, such as accountability to the poor, to the victims of violence, to children everywhere, and to witness to friends, neighbors, and colleagues.

The first anchor of accountability is the *poor of the earth,* which lies at the heart of the judgment of the nations as described in Matthew's gospel:

> Then the King will say to those at his right hand, "Come, O blessed of my Father, inherit the kingdom prepared for you from the foundation of the world; for I was hungry and you gave me food, I was thirsty and you gave me drink, I was a stranger and you welcomed me, I was naked and you clothed me, I was sick and you visited me, I was in prison and you came to me." Then the righteous will answer him, "Lord, when did we see thee hungry and feed thee, or thirsty and give thee drink? And when did we see thee a stranger and welcome thee, or naked and clothe thee? And when did we see thee sick or in prison and visit thee?" And the King will answer them, "Truly, I say to you, as you did it to one of the least of these my brethren, you did it to me."—Matthew 25:34-40 RSV

The greatness of a civilization or nation lies not in its achievements in music, science, the arts, or architecture, but rather, in how it has provided for the poor and vulnerable—the hungry, sick, imprisoned, and the immigrant. Similarly, our success in life should not be measured by the size of a home, an expensive car, the status of our occupation, or our "upward mobility." Blessedness is being accountable to the poor in our occupation, neighborhood, lifestyle, citizenship, and financial stewardship. Similarly, success for the church is measured not in increasing respectability, beautiful buildings, and steady growth in members and finance. The church is successful when it exists alongside the poor and vulnerable in slum and village and is an enabler and advocate. The viewpoint of the poor is something we in the Restoration movement understood well in our early days: "And remember in all things, the poor and the needy, the sick and the afflicted, for he that doeth not these things, the same is not my disciple" (Doctrine and Covenants 52:9c). Accountability, then—to the poor and vulnerable—is the first priority. When that is fulfilled, more will be empowered to enrich as well as enjoy those other delightful, but secondary, measures of human achievement.

The second anchor is accountability to the *victims of violence.* This, too, is a perspective we understood well in our early days when church members were persecuted, driven from their lands and homes, beaten, imprisoned, tarred and feathered, and massacred. We are called to be accountable to the prisoners of conscience, those tortured in repressive societies. We are called to be accountable to those who are victims of war and military spending. We are called to be accountable to those who are victims of economic, political, and social systems that oppress and devalue the poor, weak, and vulnerable in our own nations and abroad. Our accountability to the victims of violence will furthermore help keep us nonviolent in our advocacy for change.

The third anchor is our calling to be accountable to *little children everywhere.* The world we are building is for them to inherit. We may sometimes feel that the victims of violence and poverty deserve it, but innocent children remind us that they are the greatest victims of violence and poverty. In no way is this their just reward.

The fourth anchor is to be willing to *share with friends, colleagues, and neighbors* what we are doing and why: "It becometh every man who hath been warned to warn his neighbor" (Doctrine and Covenants 85:22a). We are accountable for sharing and inviting them to join us in discipleship for peace and justice—to know the personal God we have encountered in Jesus. Much more can be achieved when we are growing in number. The universalism of Christ is also expressed in responding to the commission of Jesus to teach all nations (Matthew 28:18-20 RSV), for all are called according to the gifts of God unto them (Doctrine and Covenants 119:8). We begin by holding ourselves accountable for those we already know.

Previously the cross has been described as the test of everything that deserves to be called Christian. Among the poor and oppressed of an occupied nation, Jesus forever reminds us of the innocents put to death. In our accountability to the poor, to the victims of violence, and to little children, we are holding ourselves accountable to the ultimate test of everything that deserves to be called Christian—the crucified Lord.

Finally, it is far more effective to be specific about accountability, to establish measurable goals and specific times of evaluation. It is a healthy practice to render an account of our finances once a year in the light of the poor, the victims of violence, little children, and our mission. To review our whole discipleship regularly in terms of time and energy with at least one other person is helpful for the warmth and strength that comes from the support and encouragement of another. Small group meetings specifically for mutual support and accountability could make all the difference in living a victorious discipleship. Larger gatherings of worship and conference will challenge, uplift, and renew those commitments we have made in baptism to the crucified and risen God.

Always a Student: Learning for Peace, Justice, and a Global View

The Restoration Christian tradition of being open to yet more light and truth is an essential aspect of effective discipleship. "Seek learning by study and by faith" (Doctrine and Covenants 85:36a) was an early admonition. Joseph Smith further indicated, under inspiration, that without scholarship Zionic community cannot be: "Study and learn, and become acquainted with all good books, and with languages, tongues and people" (Doctrine and Covenants 87:5b). Further, "It is my will that you should hasten . . . to obtain a knowledge of history, and of countries, and of kingdoms, of laws of God and man, and all this for the salvation of Zion" (Doctrine and Covenants 90:12).

However, as Paul testified, "we see through a glass darkly" (I Corinthians 13:12). In understanding the complexities of human societies our conclusions are also tentative and open to further modification in the light of experience and insight. We always have to humbly admit we could be wrong. The Restoration movement began in the spirit of open inquiry and honest questioning. Thus, Restoration Christians cannot be dogmatic idealogues of right or left. Informed by the worth of persons and an openness to truth wherever we find it, we cannot sacrifice people to the idols of fixed dogmatic positions. Human sacrifice to any idol of wood, symbol, or thought has been firmly rejected by biblical tradition since Abraham.

Yet we still need that which we can obtain through a glass darkly. If research and education are painful, expensive, and sometimes tentative, we need only be reminded that dogmatic ignorance is far more costly. Each of us needs to work at understanding the economic, social, and political structures of our global society so that we can understand the human systems that perpetuate injustice and war.

It is ironic that only in the last twenty or thirty years has peace research and education really begun. The funds and personnel are only a tiny fraction of the funds and personnel available for military research and education, yet already the beginnings are exciting. Peace research is a wedge to crack the human systems of war and violence. As we understand better the causes of war and the conditions for peace, so we can more intelligently make our contribution. Blind pacificism is not enough; in fact, it may even contribute to violence and war.

A native American proverb of unknown origin suggests "before you judge someone you must walk in his moccasins for three days." The gift of universalism in the gospel must, like all gifts, be developed if it is to be effective. To walk in the boots of the Russians, the footprints of the Pakistanis, the sandals of the Chinese, or the clogs of the Dutch gives us an experience which can help create a global perspective.

In studying and understanding other languages, histories, and cultures we begin to see more clearly our own parochialism and nationalism. In seeing and experiencing alternative ways of doing things among another people and in other cultures we may begin to become self-critical of our own. New options for living begin to emerge. Nurtured by the spirit of universalism and the equal worth of all persons, a global perspective begins to grow.

In an interdependent world threatened by global nuclear holocaust it is frightening that most of our political leaders have never lived or studied abroad. Too often, as a result, they represent the most self-centered, parochial, and nationalistic aspects of their cultures and nations.

Intercultural education for ourselves and our children is a necessity if we want to be on the forefront of a new day. Achievement of excellence need not be expensive. Many ethnic groups in our own cities retain their language and culture. They offer on our doorstep many opportunities for intercultural education. To spend a year studying in Europe or Japan may be no more expensive than a year's college in North America. To work abroad, as a student and later as a professional or tradesperson, one can cover the expenses, possibly through scholarships, grants, and exchange programs. As young people begin to experience intercultural opportunities they may mature to become citizens, parents, and workers with a global perspective which makes for peace, mutuality, and justice. From their number we shall have a new generation of leaders who in congregations, businesses, and governments will represent the best in our cultures and nations. They may be better enabled to work in the spirit of cooperation encouraging all to be winners.

Some of the world's most outstanding leaders and innovators have been students of two or more cultures. Moses was the product of three cultures—Israelite slave, Egyptian court, and desert nomad. Out of this experience—touched by the spirit of Yahweh—came the idea, strategy, and achievement of Exodus. The writer of second Isaiah, who penned perhaps the most superb insights of Judaism, wrote while exiled in Babylon. Jesus, himself the product of heaven and earth, spent his early years in Egypt before living in cosmopolitan Galilee. Paul, and many others of his day, were products of Greek and Jewish cultures. They were instrumental in establishing the church within one generation throughout the length and breadth of the Roman Empire.

Mahatma Gandhi was educated in India and England before working as a lawyer in South Africa. His innovations in nonviolent resistance were the product of his respect for law (gained from his studies of English law) and his respect for life (gained from his own Hindu religion, the Sermon on the Mount, and the writings of the Russian Tolstoy and the American Thoreau). Dr. James Yen, initiator of a mass education movement in China after World War I and later a pioneer in rural development in the Philippines, was a Chinese scholar who also studied in the United States. Albert Schweitzer—musician, theologian, missionary doctor, and Nobel Prize winner—grew up on the border between Germany and France and was fluent in both languages. Martin Luther King was a black Southern Baptist who later studied in a predominantly white, liberal New England university. The examples are numerous. The point is clear—intercultural education can help equip all of us for peace and justice.

The question is this: Is there enough time and will there be enough of us with a global perspective to make a difference? Edwin O. Reischauer, an American scholar who grew up in Japan, argues that we may have as little as twenty years.[5] Perhaps this is enough if we "hasten" to heed this ancient admonition:

> Walk together
> Talk together
> O ye peoples of the earth
> Then and only then shall ye know peace.[6]

Nonviolent Transformation

Conflict is normal and inevitable among humans, but conflict between groups is more certain and more severe. As Reinhold Niebuhr pointed out, humans in groups tend to be more selfish and less moral collectively than individually.[7] Furthermore, conflict is an imperative in the face of injustice. However, violence that terrorizes, maims, and kills is the most inadequate way of conflict resolution. More and more the victims are the innocent. The world has to be changed, but methods of transformation have to be created and used which do not betray the worth of all humans.

Violence that is expressed through social institutions or military machines threatens not just the survival of some as it has done in the past. In a nuclear age, we are all threatened by methods of conflict resolution which still belong to the age of barbarianism.

The spirit and ethic of the Sermon on the Mount, "Love your enemies," has never been more relevant or necessary than today. Its time has come, and we either disarm our enemies by love, or else we shall perish with them. In survival or in holocaust we are in fellowship with them, whatever we do.

It is appropriate to pause before going any further to reconsider violence in European culture and its heirs—the Americas, Australia, and South Africa. European culture is not unique in its violence, but it is worth looking first at ourselves before speaking in judgment of others.

The Roman Empire was violent, as any oppressed minority of Jesus' time knew. Christians were persecuted by the authorities for up to three hundred years. Then within a hundred years Christians, the persecuted, became Christians, the persecutors. The nonviolent Christian counterculture was co-opted by the surrounding Roman culture. European Christian religion became more and more indistinguishable in its violence from European culture—thus resulting in the Crusades, the inquisitions, and wars between Catholics and Protestants. Reflect upon European stewardship of the Americas. Nature, cultures, and civilizations in North, South, and Central America were plundered. So brutally successful were the Europeans in the Americas that slave labor for plantations had to be imported from Africa, resulting in the devastation of other peoples in yet another continent. In Tasmania the native people were wiped out. The story has already been told of European colonialism in India and elsewhere. Today, white South Africa demonstrates some of the worst systematic violence directly imposed on another people.

Consider economic and industrial development. The development of industrialization plundered the environment and wreaked countless horrors upon the poor and vulnerable at a time when wealth was increasing rapidly, but shared by very few. Communism, also a European invention, has tended to be violent in its reaction, using the same violence that has been inherent continuously in European culture. In war, mechanization of death was initiated by the machine gun and pogrom. Persecution of Jews and others was industrialized at Auschwitz, Dachau, and Belhauser. Our culture and civilization invented and used the atomic bomb. Today, the two polarities of European culture—the United States and the USSR—threaten to destroy us all in their violence toward each other. The perpetuation of the values of violence in our culture continues with children's war toys and children's television. By age eighteen an average child will have seen more murders than meals eaten.

When the Americans claimed their independence from the British, they did so with characteristic European violence. To remember this makes even more vivid the revolution for independence by India in 1947. It was won in large measure by the remarkable tactics of nonviolent resistance initiated by Gandhi.

It is worth summarizing here the arguments for nonviolent resistance. For the following I am indebted to Christopher Sugden:[8]

1. Nonviolent resistance expresses the Christian understanding of evil. It makes evil distinct from the evildoer. It gives an opportunity to show opponents that they are loved and respected, even if their activities are resisted. Nonviolence recognizes that people can repent.

Those choosing nonviolent resistance do so admitting their contribution to the evil prevailing. They humbly recognize they may even be wrong. In choosing a framework which not only permits the opponent to survive but also to be respected, the opponent is given the opportunity through dialogue to make a point of view known and correct the errors of the resistors.

2. Nonviolent resistance "seeks to include the opponent in a future society." It is to be a win-win victory for both sides. "Non-violent resistance presupposes that you and your opponent share a relationship which can be restored"—a perspective which is profoundly Christian.

3. Nonviolent resistance isolates and projects very clearly the issue at stake. Nonviolent resistance does not threaten the "homes, families, lives and very fabric of society." Thus, a government has to struggle to cloud the issue presented, something it can do more easily if protestors are violent and threaten to terrorize the innocent as well as the guilty. The legitimate grievances of Catholics in Northern Ireland might long ago have been met if the violent methods of the IRA had not terrorized moderate Protestants there and alienated the vast majority of the British public.

4. In the process of conflict, nonviolence gives the powerless a means of effecting political change. They may not be able to afford weapons, they have no economic muscle, they may not even have a vote, but they have their bodies. They can march, they can sit in, they can disrupt, and they can suffer. Nonviolence gives a voice to the voiceless, as even Reinhold Niebuhr conceded: "Non-violence is peculiarly

adapted to the needs and limitations of a group with more power arrayed against it, than it is able to command."

When it seems that the violent and powerful inevitably succeed in their objectives, nonviolent resistance helps us see a way for the meek to inherit the earth after all. The meek have a way with faith, further innovation, and costly suffering which can yet redeem our still-violent European cultures, whether in Europe or transplanted elsewhere.

The advocates of peace, scholars, and social innovators can speak for themselves in the following anthology and point to a wealth of insight and experience in literature elsewhere.

KENNETH BOULDING

We have achieved personal disarmament almost everywhere except in the wild parts of the world like Sicily and Texas. This happened as a result of a very complex social process; it was a disarmament race. . . just because it paid off to disarm.

I think the most important thing a [person] can do is to believe that peace is possible; and the second is to say to other people that this is so. Really the greatest obstacle to peace is the feeling that the problem is not worth working on because it is so difficult.[9]

SALLY CARRIGHER

War is not in our genes.[10]

BARBARA DEMING

Battles of any kind provoke a violent response—because those who have power are not going to give it up voluntarily. But there is simply no question that—in any long run—violent battle provokes a more violent response and brings greater casualties. . . . If the genius of guerilla warfare is to make it impossible to exploit [for an opponent] its superior brute force, non-violence can be said to carry this even further.[11]

MARGARET MEAD

Warfare is only an invention. If we despair over the way in which war seems such an ingrained habit of most of the human race, we can take comfort from the fact that a poor invention will usually give place to a better invention.

For this, two conditions at least are necessary. The people must recognize the defects of the old invention and someone must make a new one. Propaganda against warfare, documentation of its terrible cost in human suffering and social waste, these prepare the ground by teaching people to feel that warfare is a defective social institution. There is further needed a belief that social invention is possible and the invention of new methods which will render warfare as out-of-date as the tractor is making the plow or the motor car the horse and buggy. A form of behavior becomes out of date only when something else takes its place and in order to invent forms of behavior which make war obsolete it is a first requirement to believe that an invention is possible.[12]

MAHATMA GANDHI

I object to violence because when it appears to do good, the good is only temporary; the evil it does is permanent.

I do not believe in violent short-cuts to success. . . . However much I may sympathize with and admire worthy motives, I am an uncompromising opponent of violent methods even to serve the noblest of causes. . . . Experience convinces me that permanent good can never be the outcome of untruth and violence.

He who trembles or takes to his heels the moment he sees two people fighting is not nonviolent but a coward. A nonviolent person will lay down his life in preventing such quarrels.

Civil disobedience is the inherent right of a citizen. He dare not give it up without ceasing to be a man. Civil disobedience is never followed by anarchy. Criminal disobedience can lead to it. Every state puts down criminal disobedience by force. It perishes, if it does not. But to put down civil disobedience is to attempt to imprison conscience.

I hold myself to be incapable of hating any being on earth. By a long course of prayerful discipline, I have ceased for over forty years to hate anybody. I know this is a big claim. Nevertheless I make it in all humility.

But I can and do hate evil wherever it exists. I hate the system of government that the British people have set up in India. I hate the ruthless exploitation of India even as I hate from the bottom of my heart the hideous system of untouchability for which millions of Hindus have made themselves responsible. But I do not hate the domineering Englishmen as I refuse to hate the domineering Hindus. I seek to reform them in all the loving ways that are open to me. My noncooperation has its roots not in hatred, but in love.

I believe that if one man gains spiritually the whole world gains with him and, if one man falls, the whole world falls to that extent. I do not help opponents without at the same time helping myself and my co-workers.

For a nonviolent person, the whole world is one family. He will thus fear none, nor will others fear him.[13]

MARTIN LUTHER KING

Violence brings only temporary victories; violence by creating many more social problems than it solves never brings permanent peace. . . . A voice echoing through the corridors of time, says to every intemperate Peter, "Put up thy sword." History is cluttered with the wreckage of nations that failed to follow Christ's command.

Only through an inner spiritual transformation do we gain the strength to fight vigorously the evils of the world in a humble and loving spirit. The transformed non-conformist, moreover, never yields to the passive sort of patience which is an excuse to do nothing. And his very transformation saves him from speaking irresponsible words which estrange without reconciling and from making hasty judgments which are blind to the necessity of social progress. He recognizes that social change will not come overnight, yet he works as though it is an imminent possibility.

Returning hate for hate multiplies hate, adding deeper darkness to a night already devoid of stars. Darkness cannot drive out darkness, only light can do that. Hate cannot drive out hate, only love can do that.

Time is cluttered with the wreckage of communities which surrender to hatred and violence. For the salvation of our nation and the salvation of mankind we must follow another way. This does not mean we abandon our righteous efforts. With every ounce of our energy we must continue to rid this nation of the incubus of segregation. But we shall not in the process relinquish our privilege and our obligation to love. While abhorring segregation, we shall love the segregationalist. This is the only way to create the beloved community.

To our most bitter opponents we say: "We shall match your capacity to inflict suffering by our capacity to endure suffering. We shall meet your physical force with soul force. Do to us what you will and we shall continue to love you. We cannot in all good conscience obey your unjust laws, because non-cooperation with evil is as much a moral obligation as is cooperation with good. Throw us in jail, and we shall love you. Bomb our homes and threaten our children, and we shall still love you. Send your hooded perpetrators of violence into our community at the midnight hour and beat us and leave us half dead, and we shall still love you. But be assured that we shall wear you down by our capacity to suffer. One day we shall win freedom, but not only for ourselves. We shall so appeal to your heart and conscience that we shall win you in the process and our victory will be a double victory."[14]

JAN LOCHMAN, CZECH THEOLOGIAN

It is only through ecumenical solidarity with the hungry, oppressed people in the developing countries, and by supporting their justified revolutionary demands, that the privileged Christians of Europe today can make a testimony of non-violent love which will carry any conviction.[15]

On the Forefront

We live in a moment of history when radically new possibilities are opening before us. Possibilities for freedom or bondage, creation or destruction. And the power is within our hands to decide which direction the history of civilization will take. This power to decide is the sign of what it means to be alive today.[16]

You who are my disciples must be found continuing in the forefront of those organizations and movements which are recognizing the worth of persons and are committed to bringing the ministry of my Son to bear on their lives.—Doctrine and Covenants 151:9

We are few in numbers; our resources seem scanty;

our commitment often fitful. To be effective we need to be converted and—with God's help—understand through study, faith, and action where the forefront issues of our day are. It is here, where today is becoming tomorrow, that the few with vision, inspired strategy, and effective action can make the greatest impact. Our conversion has to be related to the social and political realities of our day. Some major forefronts have been indicated—they are wherever it is recognized that the worth of persons is being violated. As we move from the agricultural and industrial age to the information age this will happen in new ways. Whether we work *against* poverty, war, racism, or *for* sexual equality or peace, it matters not. To work in one is to participate in the struggle for all, for they are all interrelated.

Perhaps we do not know where to begin. Today is becoming tomorrow in us and our children. We can begin here. The forefront is us and we are inseparably connected through our ecology of systems and institutions to vitually everyone else on this earth. The forefront is us; God can make the world a better place if I let God begin with me and accept my unique and precious worth in God's sight.

We can go on to find others, in our neighborhood, in our city, and beyond for we shall not be alone. In the dark, awful days of World War I, Elbert A. Smith spoke to our people words of prophetic counsel that are still relevant with a spirit that transcends times and place.

> Again, at this time you are admonished that you be not unduly concerned because you are few in number as compared with the world. That is not your concern, but be concerned only that your righteousness shall be very great. For a few righteous [people] can accomplish very much, and a little leaven leaveneth a great lump.

> I have many forces at work in the world, saith the Lord, I have many spiritual forces at work that you know not of. You see but the smaller part of my work, and the world perceives it not at all.
>
> Therefore be not concerned because you are few in number, but. . .look to [yourself], and to the condition of [your] own heart and life. Be humble and righteous and full of love, casting out the spirit of hatred, that you may stand in holy places and receive the blessings of the Lord.[17]

We are few, but not alone. It is time for us to begin to know other individuals and organizations outside our tradition with whom we can work to make a difference in changing institutions and systems into the kingdom of justice and peace. What we have to share can be of great help to others too. Together we can intentionally be part of a bigger plan. And around the globe, little children—hungry, sick, and afraid—are depending on us to make that difference.

STUDY QUESTIONS

1. a. Do you think you should be accountable for your lifestyle to the poor, victims of violence, and little children?
   b. If you want to be accountable in this way, how would you go about it?
   c. Would you risk holding yourself accountable to others you trust, about finances, your job, where and how you live? What would help you make the step? What would hinder you?
2. What intercultural experiences have you had? What were some of the growing pains you encountered?
3. a. How would you feel about helping one of your children to live abroad to study or work as a young adult?
   b. What are some of the risk, pain, and costs involved for the young person and for yourself?
   c. What gains are there in terms of increased maturity, enlarged vision, and career development?
4. One of the major tensions in the church today is between those of a global vision and those of a more local perspective. In conflicts that arise between these two groups, how can the interests of each group be honored?
5. Nonviolent transformation is a major theme throughout this book. Martin Luther King gave the following as preparation for a nonviolent campaign:

> In any non-violent campaign there are four basic steps: collection of the facts to determine whether injustices exist; negotiation; self-purification; and direct action. . . . Nonviolent direct action seeks to create such a crisis and foster

such a tension that a community which has refused to negotiate is forced to confront the issue.

—Letter from Birmingham Jail, April 1963

How would you feel about nonviolent direct action

a. as an observer?

b. as a supporter in the wings?

c. as a participant?

6. a. Our tradition has long had a healthy respect for the laws of the land. Are there any circumstances when faithfulness requires breaking human law or should one always be obedient to a government?

   b. Does civil disobedience promote anarchy and disorder or facilitate peaceful change? How is civil disobedience different from criminal disobedience?

7. In what ways could you join with others to be leaven

   a. in the church?

   b. in your neighborhood?

   c. as citizens in your nation?

8. This study course is ended. What do you plan to actually commit yourself to doing?

NOTES

1. Paul Nelson, class, *Bread for the World Educational Fund Seminar,* RLDS Central Congregation, Kansas City, April 19, 1985.
2. Martin Luther King, *Strength to Love* (Glasgow: Collins Fortana Paperbacks, reprinted 1984), 24.
3. Brock Chisholm, cited in Norman Z. Alcock, *The Bridge of Reason* (Toronto: Canadian Peace Research Institute, 1961), 3.
4. E. F. Schumacher, *Good Work* (London: Abacus Paperbacks, 1980), 140.
5. See Edwin O. Reischauer, *Toward the 21st Century: Education for a Changing World* (New York: Random House, 1974).
6. Source unknown.
7. Reinhold Niebuhr, *Moral Man and Immoral Society* (New York: Scribner, 1960).
8. Christopher Sugden, *A Different Dream: Non-violence as Practical Politics* (Bramcote, Nottingham, England: Grove Books, 1976), 15, 16.
9. Kenneth Boulding, cited in Peter van der Dungen, *Foundations of Peace Research* (University of Bradford: Peace Studies Papers Number 1, 1980), 45.
10. Sally Carrigher, cited in van der Dungen, 53
11. Barbara Deming, "Non-violence and Casualties" in C. R. Beitz and T. Herman, eds., *Peace and War* (San Francisco: W. H. Freeman and Co., 1973), 377.
12. Margaret Mead, "Warfare Is Only an Invention" in Beitz and Herman, 117, 118.
13. Eknath Easwaran, *Gandhi the Man,* second edition (Petaluma, California: Nilgiri Press, 1978), 42, 43, 90, 43, 56, 75, 115.
14. King, 14, 15, 23, 51, 54, 55.
15. J. M. Lochman, cited in John Ferguson, *The Politics of Love: The New Testament and Non-violent Revolution* (Cambridge: Clarke & Co., 1982 reprint), 50.
16. Source unknown.
17. *Saints' Herald* 64, no. 46 (November 14, 1917): 1081.

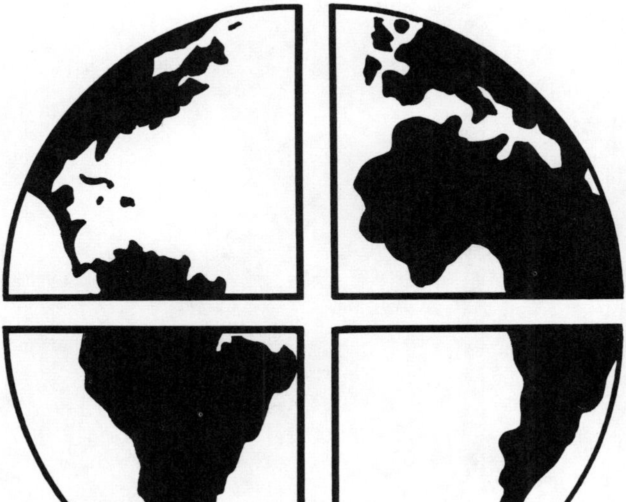